ACCLAIM FOR THE ESOP COACH

"Kelly Finnell has filled a vacuum in ESOP literature – he has come up with a handbook for business owners that explains the complex subject in clear, direct and understandable terms. Everything the reader needs to master the ESOP technique is there, but with the usual technical jargon and arcane legal references stripped away. Anyone thinking about liquidity options for their business should read this book before making any final decisions."

Jared Kaplan, Esq.
McDermott Will & Emery, Senior Counsel
Co-author, *BNA Tax Portfolio on ESOPs*

"Kelly Finnell's long experience in the ESOP world makes him very well qualified to explain how this too-often overlooked approach to business transition works. ESOPs were designed by Congress to provide unique tax advantages to owners, companies, and employees, advantages no other approach can replicate. Just as important, ESOPs provide a way for business owners to exit gradually or quickly, pass on ownership to the people who helped build the business, and maintain the independence of the company they have worked so hard to build. ESOPs are not right for everyone, but Kelly Finnell's important book can help you determine if they are right for you."

Corey Rosen, Ph.D.
Executive Director
National Center for Employee Ownership

"An ESOP is one of the greatest instruments of US capitalism. I've seen ESOPs used successfully by a number of companies in our industry. I would recommend this book to anyone interested in learning how an ESOP could help with their company's ownership succession planning."

Dominic Pileggi
Chairman & CEO, Thomas & Betts

i

"I have great admiration for anyone who can master an area of subject matter, distill it into understandable form, and present it to the public in a fine book. Kelly Finnell has done just that! This book on ESOPs will tell you everything you need to know to rationally consider the option, and, if you choose, execute the plan. Kelly's treatise is the best on this topic - If you are a business owner, this is a must-read book!"

Don Hutson
Speaker and co-author of *The New York Times* and
The Wall Street Journal #1 Best-Seller, *The One Minute Entrepreneur*

"Kelly has taken a topic which is a mystery to most of us -- use of an ESOP to effect an ownership change -- and explains it in an understandable and "plain English" manner. The book's examples are instructive and understandable and will help readers quickly decide if this is a strategy which is right for them."

Wade McKnight, CPA
Retired Partner, Deloitte

"Take it from the author of *Public Speaking*, if you're looking for an informative and understandable speaker on ESOPs, Kelly Finnell is your man."

Michael Osborn, Ph.D.
Professor of Communication
Co-author, *Public Speaking*

"Kelly Finnell has delivered his promise; he has taken a complicated issue and broken it down into understandable pieces. As an entrepreneur and small business owner, I find the options that Kelly provides make for both informative and enjoyable reading. This is must reading for the small to mid-sized business owner."

Ed Horrell
Author, *The Kindness Revolution*

"The ESOP Coach provides valuable insight on the complex issues of business succession, presenting the information in an easy to understand manner. Kelly has excellent perspective on the challenges and opportunities, which makes The ESOP Coach essential reading for business owners (and their advisors) focused on the ongoing success of the businesses they have built and preserving the entrepreneurial spirit that remains the backbone of our country."

Fred Jonske, FSA, MAAA
CEO, M Financial Group

"I've often thought that the main reason an ESOP is not more frequently used in Exit Planning for owners is its apparent complexity in design and implementation. As Winston Churchill once said in a different context, "The length of this document defends it well against the risk of its being read." And so it can be with the mass of ESOP explanations, rules and regulations. Kelly succeeds in his avowed purpose of providing a straightforward and understandable explanation of this important planning tool. His book is well worth reading for every owner considering a business exit."

John H. Brown
President
Business Enterprise Institute
Author of *How To Run Your Business So You Can Leave It In Style*
and Co-author of *Cash Out Move On*

"This book has a wealth of information to help business owners make intelligent decisions about whether they should use an ESOP as part of their ownership succession planning. It has all of the technical information you need as well as user-friendly explanations and illustrative case studies. There is certainly something here for everyone."

Pete Prodoehl
Vice President, Principal Financial Group

"Kelly and I have had the opportunity to work together with a number of business owners over the years to help design the right transition or exit plan for each situation. The ESOP is one of the key alternatives we discuss, since it brings so many business and tax advantages to the table. What distinguishes Kelly from other ESOP advisors is his ability to explain the ESOP strategy in a way that is simple to understand and which is on point with the needs of the business owner. Through this book, Kelly is sharing the insights he and his team have gained through the many years which they have specialized in this field. Kelly and I share a common objective in our transition and exit planning practices, which is to help business owners beat the odds by achieving the legacy they wish to achieve. I am glad to see Kelly share these important ESOP strategies with both business owners and with other exit planning advisors."

Nicholas K. Niemann, Esq.
McGrath North Law Firm
Author, *Exit On Your Terms*

Kelly O. Finnell, J.D., CLU, AIF®

The
ESOP
Employee Stock Ownership Plan
COACH

Using ESOPs in Ownership Succession Planning

EXECUTIVE FINANCAL SERVICES, INC.

Copyright 2010

Kelly O. Finnell, J. D., CLU, AIF®

ISBN 978-0-578-04699-0

DISCLAIMER

While the examples mentioned in this book are based on actual clients' situations, the names and facts have been changed in order to protect their privacy. This publication should not be considered as legal, tax, business or financial advice. This publication is designed to provide information about the subject matter covered. It is provided with the understanding that while the author is a licensed attorney, he has not been engaged by the reader to render legal or other professional services (unless a specific engagement agreement has been executed). If legal advice or other expert assistance is required by the reader, the services of a competent professional should be sought. The author shall not have any liability or responsibility to any person or entity with respect to any loss or damage caused, or alleged to be caused, directly or indirectly, by the information contained in this book. While this book contains information which is intended to be thorough, the author does not presume to address every conceivable matter which could impact a particular business owner's exit situation. Use of this book by the reader constitutes agreement to these terms.

Circular 230 Disclosure

The following statement is required by U. S. Treasury Department Regulations: Any U. S. tax advice contained in this communication is not intended or written to be used, and cannot be used, for the purpose of (i) avoiding penalties under the Internal Revenue Code or (ii) promoting, marketing or recommending to another party any transaction or matter addressed herein.

Author Contact Information:
Kelly O. Finnell, J. D., CLU, AIF®
Executive Financial Services, Inc.
7660 Poplar Pike, 2nd Floor
Germantown, TN 38138
(901) 259-7979
kfin@execfin.com
www.execfin.com
www.ESOPcoach.com

DEDICATION

This book is dedicated to my family.

To my mother who taught me to read.

To my father who constantly told me I could do anything
I set my mind to.

To my wife who taught me the meaning of love and compassion.

To my daughters who have brought unimaginable joy into my life.

ACKNOWLEDGEMENTS

I would like to acknowledge and thank the following people for their assistance with this book.

The members of my Firm who have assisted and supported me in this project: Keyonlia Narcisse, MBA, Ben Schultz and Ben Buffington.

Jeff McGoff, J.D., LLM, Alfred L. Jones, CPA, and especially Kimberly Moore for their feedback on the manuscript.

Corey Rosen, Executive Director of the National Center for Employee Ownership (nceo.org) for permission to reprint excerpts from the NCEO's "ESOP Q&A."

Most of all I'd like to thank Susan Drake of Spellbinders, Inc. for coaching me through the process of writing my first book. Without her advice and editing this book would not have been possible. She helped me "find my voice" and supported me throughout this project.

ESOP COACH

TABLE OF CONTENTS

FOREWORD

I remember telling my golf coach that he had a unique ability to communicate a single concept a dozen different ways until he finally explained it so even I could understand it. That ability to communicate a concept that is second nature to the coach in a way so that it connects with the student is the essence of good coaching.

That is what I try to accomplish in this book. I attempt to take a very complex topic (Employee Stock Ownership Plan or "ESOP") and explain it in such a way that someone who is a novice to the topic can grasp it.

I do this by describing what an ESOP is and how it works as I would if I were sitting across from you at your desk. I use plain English and some charts.

I don't give you all of the details at first. I assume that when you ask me what time it is, you want to hear "4:50 pm" rather than a detailed explanation of how the watch was made.

However, as they say, "the devil is in the detail." Therefore, I have notated my initial explanation of an ESOP referencing the subsequent chapters that give you all of the detail most business owners could ever want. What you will find in these subsequent chapters is a "Q&A" format that will allow you to focus on those questions that are most pertinent to your situation rather than having to read an entire chapter to find the one paragraph that answers your question.

I hope you find my unique approach to coaching you through the ESOP process to be helpful.

Kelly Finnell
The ESOP Coach

PREFACE

If you are one of the 78.2 million Americans born between 1946 and 1964 (the "Baby Boom" generation) and if you own a business ("Baby Boomer Business Owner"), this book was written for you. I'm a Boomer too, and I've always believed we are a group without limits; people undaunted by challenges and quick to grab opportunity.

Now here we are, near retirement age, and we face a difficult dilemma. Most of us will need to use some or all of the wealth we have created in our business to fund our lifestyle during retirement. Historically, people in this situation have had to sell their business to get the funds for a secure and enjoyable retirement.

Selling a business can certainly yield money; on the other hand, there can be enormous sacrifices in both financial and personal areas. Things associated with a sale, like taxes, loss of control, loss of a legacy and others may have a devastating impact.

So here's the dilemma: bluntly put, do you want to walk away from the work of your life and pay a huge amount of tax for the privilege?

Many Boomers would say "no" if only they had an alternative. Fortunately, you have a desirable option: an Employee Stock Ownership Plan (ESOP). An ESOP is one of the most powerful planning strategies ever created by the United States Congress. An ESOP lets you get the money you need – and deserve – for retirement without surrendering control of your business or paying exorbitant taxes.

Over the past 30 years I have worked with thousands of Baby Boomer Business Owners. Each one of them is unique in the way they operate their business and plan for its future. I've written this book with that in mind.

Here are some ways you can use this book.

- If you are a detail-oriented person who wants to know all of the intricacies of ESOPs, you may want to read this book from cover-to-cover.

- If you are a conceptual thinker who wants a "40,000-foot view" of ESOPs and succession planning, you may want to read Chapter 1, which will provide an overview of your Succession Planning options, and then skip to Chapter 3 for an assessment of which option may work best for you.

- If you fall somewhere between these two extremes, you may want to read the first three chapters, read the case studies that most resemble your situation and then read just the Q&As in which you have a particular interest.

Boomers, take charge. The time to plan is now. Your company will be a critical component of your personal and financial legacy. Don't leave it to chance.

I hope that some of these quotations will inspire you to start planning today.

The nicest thing about not planning is that failure comes as a complete surprise, rather than being preceded by a period of worry and depression.
-Sir John Henry James

You should work on your business, just not in your business.
-Michael Gerber

By failing to prepare, you are preparing to fail.
-Benjamin Franklin

Plans are only good intentions unless they immediately degenerate into hard work.
-Peter Drucker

It pays to plan ahead. It wasn't raining when Noah built the ark.
-Unknown

1

INTRODUCING THE ESOP AS AN OWNERSHIP SUCCESSION PLANNING STRATEGY

*T*raditionally, there have been three options for owners to consider relative to their succession planning: sell to an Outsider, sell to an Insider or what we call a "till death do us part" strategy. Despite the availability of ESOPs as an ownership succession strategy for more than 35 years, few business owners are aware of this option and its many benefits.

Each of the succession planning strategies mentioned above can be the best fit based upon a business owner's situation and goals. In the next chapter, we will discuss the pros and cons of each of these options. In this chapter, I will introduce you to ESOPs as an Ownership Succession Strategy.

WHAT IS AN ESOP?

There are three different parties or constituencies involved in ESOPs and the answer to this question depends upon which constituency's perspective you consider.

- To an owner of a closely held company, an ESOP is a way to get money out of his company on a tax-advantaged basis and to transition control of his company to key employees or family (Insiders).
- To a company's employees, an ESOP is a retirement plan (like a 401k) that allows employees to share in the value of their company.
- To a company, an ESOP is a vehicle of corporate finance that offers

tax benefits not available anywhere else in the Internal Revenue Code.

HOW DOES AN ESOP WORK?

An ESOP works in many respects like any other type of qualified retirement plan such as a 401k (see Chapter 8). But there are three distinct differences between an ESOP and every other type of qualified retirement plan. And it is these differences that make an ESOP work so effectively as an ownership succession strategy.

- An ESOP can borrow money.
- It can engage in transactions with parties in interest. In this case, "parties in interest" would be the owner or owners of the business.
- An ESOP is required to invest primarily in the stock of the Company that sponsors the plan.

The following chart and step-by-step description illustrate how stock is sold to an ESOP in a typical Ownership Succession Planning scenario:

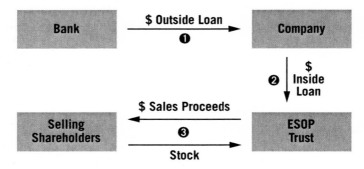

In Step 1, the company obtains a loan, often from its current bank. This is referred to as the "Outside Loan." Due to technicalities in the lending laws, banks almost never loan money directly to an ESOP. Instead, banks loan money to the company which then lends it to the ESOP.

In Step 2, the company lends money to the ESOP. Generally, the company loans the same amount it borrowed from the bank in Step 1, although the company could lend the ESOP more or less. This is referred to as the "Inside Loan." The terms (repayment period, interest rate, etc.)

of the Inside Loan often mirror the terms of the Outside Loan but there may be reasons, in certain situations, for the terms of the Inside Loan to be different from the Outside Loan.

In Step 3, the ESOP Trust, or ESOT, uses the cash it received in the Inside Loan to purchase company stock from the selling shareholder(s). The stock that is purchased will be held initially in the ESOT's "Suspense Account."

The details of ESOP Loans and the ESOT Suspense Account are explained in the Q&As contained in Chapter 9.

The following chart and the step-by-step description illustrate the annual activities involved in an ESOP.

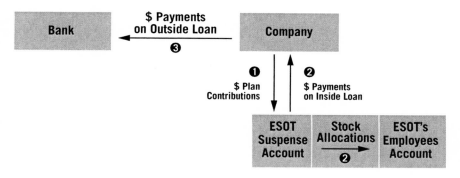

In Step 1, the Company makes a contribution to the ESOT. As with contributions to any Company sponsored retirement plan, these contributions are a tax deductible expense if certain requirements are satisfied.

In Step 2, the ESOT uses the cash it received from the Company in Step 1 and makes payments on the Inside Loan. As annual payments are made on the Inside Loan, shares are released from the ESOT Suspense Account and are allocated to employees' retirement accounts. The Company then uses the cash it received in Step 2 to make payment on the Outside Loan in Step 3.

WHAT ARE THE ESOP TAX INCENTIVES?

Owners who sell stock to an ESOP will pay tax at the 15% federal long-term capital gains tax rate (worst case scenario). If the company is a C corporation, the seller(s) may be able to defer tax, perhaps even permanently (see Chapter 10).

Employees participating in the ESOP are not taxed on the stock allocated to their accounts or on its earnings until distributed, generally at death, disability, retirement or termination of service (subject to vesting).

Companies that sponsor ESOPs are able to deduct ESOP contributions (subject to certain limitations explained in Chapter 8 Q&As 13-24). This results in a company converting what would have been a non-tax deductible principal payment on a loan into a tax deductible retirement plan contribution. This tax benefit is available for C and S corporations.

C corporations also are able to deduct dividends paid on ESOP-held stock under certain conditions (see Chapter 9 Q&A 34). This is the only way a company can get a tax deduction for dividend payments and it may allow a company an avenue to get money into its ESOP in excess of the contribution limits referenced above.

S corporations that sponsor ESOPs enjoy a unique tax benefit. For tax purposes, S corporations are "flow-through" entities, which means that they do not pay tax. Instead, their income "flows through" to their owners who include their share of the company's taxable income on their tax returns (see introduction to Chapter 11). Let's follow an S corporation through the process.

- Assume an S corporation has $5 million of taxable income and two equal shareholders. Each of the shareholders would receive an IRS form K-1 for $2.5 million.
- Assuming that they pay tax at the 35% federal tax rate, each of them would pay $875,000 in federal income tax on the S corporation earnings.
- However, since an ESOT, like all qualified retirement plan trusts is tax exempt, its portion of the Company's income is free from taxation.

- Therefore, in the example above, if an ESOP were one of the two owners, the tax liability on the Company's income would be reduced in half, saving $875,000.
- If an ESOP owned all of the Company in this example, the Company's $5 million of taxable income would be completely free from federal income tax, saving $1.75 million in income taxes.

As can be seen, Congress has created powerful tax incentives for business owners to use ESOPs as an ownership succession planning vehicle.

ESOP COACH

2

ESOP COMPARED TO OTHER STRATEGIES

*T*here are three traditional Ownership Succession Strategies: Sell to an Insider, Sell to an Outsider and "till death do us part." In this chapter, I will discuss each of these traditional options and compare each of them to an ESOP. I have summarized this comparison in our copyrighted "Ownership Succession Planning Matrix," which can be found in Appendix A.

SELL TO AN INSIDER

"Insiders" refers to a company's current employees and to the current owner's family members. In many closely held companies, family members (sons, daughters, brothers, sisters, etc.) and/or employees who are most important to the company's success are the Insiders who will take over the business when the owner leaves.

In my experience, Insiders almost never have the cash and/or credit that is needed to purchase the company. Therefore, if they are to purchase the company, the acquisition must be "boot strapped." This is where the company bonuses them the cash that is needed for the purchase. Unfortunately, the tax-bite involved in this process makes it very financially inefficient.

The following chart assumes that an Insider wants to purchase stock valued at $10 million from a current owner. The Insider will either borrow $10 million from a bank with the company as a guarantor; or the current owner will sell to the Insider for a $10 million promissory note guaranteed by the company. In either case, the company will bonus the Insider the cash he or she needs each year to service the debt. The following chart illustrates the company cash flow that is required in order for the Insider to have $10 million net after-tax to pay the selling shareholder.

Total Bonuses Paid	$15,384,615
Taxes Paid on Bonuses	$ 5,384,615
Net Remaining	$10,000,000

As you can see from this chart, because the Insider needs $10 million to service the debt and since the bonuses he receives are taxable to him, the company must bonus him $15,384,615 in order for him to have the $10 million net. Therefore, this structure requires 53% more company cash flow due to the tax bite.

Here is the math used in this chart:

$10,000,000 ÷ .65 = $15,384,615.

$10,000,000 is the amount needed to service the acquisition loan.

.65 is 100 minus the Insiders' tax rate (.35).

Using an ESOP as the purchaser "on behalf of" the Insider, saves $5,384,6315. This is the result of two things:

- the company receiving a tax deduction for the ESOP contribution used to service the acquisition debt, and
- the Insider not having to pay tax on the $10 million the company contributes to the ESOP. This 53% cost savings makes an ESOP a much more financially efficient strategy than a traditional sale to an Insider.

SELL TO AN OUTSIDER

"Outsider" refers to several types of potential buyers, including: competitors, private equity groups (PEGs), suppliers, individual investors, etc. There are many advantages to selling to an Outsider but these advantages are not as attractive as they may first appear. In fact, according to one source, 75% of people who sold their company to an Outsider later regretted their decision. Below I have listed the major benefits of selling to an Outsider with some of the caveats you should consider.

Cash Out and Move On

Many business owners assume that when they sell their company they will receive cash at closing and will be able to retire the next day. That is almost never the case. Buyers want to make sure that the company they are purchasing will continue to grow and prosper after closing. In order to protect themselves from a negative surprise, purchasers often structure sales agreements containing some or all of the following provisions: earn-outs, escrows/holdbacks, consulting/employment agreements and covenants not to compete.

Earn-outs are designed to protect a purchaser from overpaying for the company it is buying. Purchasers are almost always buying a company's future cash flow. If a purchaser expects a company's future cash flow to be $2 million per year, the purchaser might agree to pay $10,000,000 for the company. If the company's cash flow drops to $1 million per year immediately after the sale is consummated, the purchaser will have paid two times the cash flow multiple it anticipated ($10,000,000 purchase price/$1,000,000 cash flow results in a valuation multiple of 10x instead of the 5x multiple the purchaser intended to pay).

Here is how a purchaser could have protected himself from over-paying in the above example. Instead of agreeing to pay 5 times cash flow at closing, the purchase agreement could have included an earn-out provision. A purchase agreement with an earn-out might be structured as follows:

1. The purchaser agrees to pay 2.5 times the 3 previous years' average annual cash flow at closing. Assuming annual cash flow of $2 million over the previous 3 years, the purchaser will pay $5 million at closing.

2. The purchase agreement in this example may state that the purchaser will make payments on the first two anniversaries of the closing of the sale ("earn-out payments"). The purchase agreement

may state that on each anniversary if the previous year's cash flow is $1 million -$2 million the earn-out payment will equal 2.5 times the amount in excess of $1 million. The earn-out formula would be:

(Cash flow - $1,000,000) * 2.5

The purchase agreement may further state that if cash flows exceed $2 million, the earn-out payment will be calculated as follows:

$2,500,000 + (Cash flow - $2,000,000) * 1.5

The $2.5 million would be the earn-out payment on the first $2 million of cash flow. This second payment at (1.5x) would generally be referred to as a "bonus" earn-out payment.

If cash flow is less than $1 million, no earn-out payments would be made. Several examples are shown below.

If the company continues to have $2 million of cash flow following the sale, the Sellers would receive the following payments:

Closing Payment	(2.5 x $2,000,000)	$ 5,000,000
1st Anniversary	($2,000,000 - $1,000,000) * 2.5	$ 2,500,000
2nd Anniversary	($2,000,000 - $1,000,000) * 2.5	$ 2,500,000
Total Purchase Price		$10,000,000
Purchase Price/Average Annual Cash Flow		5

If the company has cash flow of $1.5 million the first year following the closing of the sale and $1.2 million the second year following closing, the Sellers would receive the following payments:

Closing Payment	(2.5 x $2,000,000)	$ 5,000,000
1st Anniversary	($1,500,000 - $1,000,000) * 2.5	$ 1,250,000
2nd Anniversary	($1,200,000 - $1,000,000) * 2.5	$ 500,000
	Total Purchase Price	$ 6,750,000
Purchase Price/Average Annual Cash Flow		5

In this case the purchaser would have successfully protected itself using an earn-out provision. Cash flow over the 2 years following the sale averaged $1,350,000. The purchaser paid $6,750,000 for the company resulting in it paying a multiple of 5-times post-sale average annual cash flow ($6,750,000 ÷ $1,350,000 = 5).

If the company's cash flow decreased to $1 million or less after the sale, the purchaser would not make any payments following the closing payment of $5 million.

If the company's cash flow increased to $3 million per year for the 2-years following closing, the Seller would receive the following payments:

Closing Payment (2.5 x $2,000,000)	$ 5,000,000
1st Anniversary ($2,500,000 +	
($3,000,000 - $2,000,000) * 1.5)	$ 4,000,000
2nd Anniversary (same as 1st above)	$ 4,000,000
Total Purchase Price	$13,000,000
Purchase Price/Average Annual Cash Flow	4.33

In this case the purchaser paid $3 million more than it would have paid without the earn-out but its purchase price multiple would be less than the 5x it was willing to pay for the company's future cash flow. The Sellers also would have benefited by receiving the additional $3 million. This earn-out formula with a bonus payment for "excess cash flow" was a good deal for both parties.

There are many ways to structure earn-outs and this is just one example. My point is not that your earn-out will be structured as illustrated above. Rather my point is that purchasers are very careful not to overpay for a company and, as a result, your sales agreement is likely to contain an earn-out, particularly when a purchase price cannot be agreed upon. Therefore, when you sell to an Outsider, you probably will not be able to cash-out and move on immediately following the sale.

Sales agreements almost always include "representation and warranties" in which the seller states certain facts about the condition of the business. If these facts later turn out not to be accurate, the purchaser may have a financial claim against the seller. To streamline collecting on this financial claim and avoid having to bring suit against the seller for the amount claimed, a portion of the sales proceeds may be placed in escrow at closing. A typical escrow amount is 10 percent. A typical escrow period is 2 years.

Here is how an escrow might impact the timing of payments in the scenario described above.

- The seller would receive $1.5 million at closing instead of $2.5 million;
- $1 million would be placed in escrow by the purchaser;
- The seller would be paid the $1 million escrow amount in 2 years when the escrow period expires (if the purchaser does not make a claim against the escrow).

Escrows present an additional hurdle to sellers being able to cash out and move on immediately following a sale.

Sales agreements generally include provisions preventing the seller from competing against the purchaser or "pirating" the company's customers. In addition, sales agreements often contain provisions requiring the seller to work for the company for 1-3 years following the sale. This prevents the seller from retiring immediately after the sale is closed.

Sometimes people say that they do not want to do an ESOP because it will not allow them to exit their company immediately following the sale. While this is true, the same can be said about a sale to an Outsider. Owners of closely held companies are almost never able to sell their company and walk away regardless of whether they sell to an Insider, an Outsider or an ESOP.

Taxes

Most business owners know that if they sell stock that they've owned for at least one year, they will pay tax at long-term capital gain tax rates rather than at ordinary income tax rates. Currently, the federal long-term capital gains tax rate is 15% and the maximum ordinary income tax rate is 35%. Therefore, being able to pay tax at the capital gains tax rate results in a savings of 57%.

Many business owners assume that when they sell their company they will pay long-term capital gains tax on the sales proceeds and will enjoy the tax savings described above. However, this often is not the case.

The taxation of proceeds from the sale of a company will depend on several factors. The principal factors are:

- whether the sale is structured as a stock sale or an asset sale; and
- whether the company is a C corporation or a "pass-through" entity such as an S corporation or LLC (Limited Liability Company).

If the sale is structured as a sale of stock, the tax consequences will be the same regardless of whether the company is a C corporation or an S corporation: The sellers will pay long-term capital gains tax on the amount of sales proceeds they receive in excess of their tax basis. Obviously, this is the best possible result for the sellers. However, purchasers almost always prefer purchasing a company's assets rather than its stock.

The first reason acquirers prefer purchasing assets is because when doing so they only assume liabilities directly associated with those assets – such as mortgages. If an acquirer purchases a company's stock, the acquirer assumes all of the company's liabilities – known and unknown. This includes errors and omissions, product liability, environmental, etc. In a small transaction (less than $100 million) the cost of due diligence to assure that there are no such liabilities is not justified by the size of the deal. Therefore, most potential acquirers will insist on purchasing assets.

The second reason acquirers prefer purchasing assets is that doing so increases the acquirer's tax benefits. This tax advantage is best illustrated by an example.

- Assume that an acquirer pays seller $10 million for company stock. The assets of the purchased company will retain the same tax basis they had prior to the acquisition.
- Assume that the total tax basis of all the assets was $3 million. The acquirer has paid $10 million, but has a tax basis in the company's assets for depreciation purposes of $3 million.

- If the purchaser had purchased the company's assets, the tax basis of those assets would have been "stepped-up;" i.e., increased to the amount paid for each asset. This could increase the acquirer's future tax benefits on the depreciation of these assets dramatically. (Please note that a stock sale coupled with a Section 338 election may achieve virtually the same result, depending on the circumstances).

If the sale is structured as an asset sale, the tax consequences to the seller will depend upon whether the company is a C corporation or a pass through entity.

If it is a C corporation, the tax consequences of an asset sale can be confiscatory. In an asset purchase, the sales agreement is between the purchaser and the company – not the purchaser and the shareholders. If the purchaser pays $10 million for the company's assets, the payment is made to the company, not the shareholders.

C corporations (unlike their shareholders) pay tax on the sale of assets at ordinary income tax rates (potentially 38%) rather than capital gains rates (15%). After a C corporation has received the sales proceeds and paid the tax associated with the sale, it then distributes the net amount to its shareholders who pay the 15% rate on "qualified dividends." This results in a double layer of tax. The chart below shows the total tax liability on a C corporation asset sale followed by a shareholder distribution.

Asset Sales Proceeds	$10,000,000
Assets' Tax Basis	$ 3,000,000
Taxable Gain	$ 7,000,000
C Corporation Tax (38%)	$ 2,660,000
Net Distribution to Shareholders	$ 7,340,000
Shareholder Tax (15%)	$ 1,101,000
Net Sales Proceeds	$ 6,239,000

Now you understand what I meant when I said earlier that a C corporation asset sale can result in a confiscatory rate of tax – in this example over 38% of the sales proceeds and approximately 53% of the taxable gain will be paid in taxes.

If the company is a pass-through entity (S corporation, partnership, or LLC), an asset sale results in far less tax. This is due to the fact that since pass-through entities do not pay federal tax, there is only one rather than two levels of taxation. Whether the tax will be at ordinary income tax rates or at capital gains tax rates will depend upon the asset being sold.

Returning to our earlier example of a $10 million company, let's "drill down" and look at the assets it owns.

	Basis	FMV	Gain	Tax
Accounts Receivable	$ 0	$ 1,000,000	$ 1,000,000[1]	$ 350,000
Inventory	$1,000,000	$ 2,000,000	$ 1,000,000[1]	$ 350,000
Warehouse	$1,500,000	$ 4,500,000	$ 3,000,000[2]	$ 450,000
Land	$ 500,000	$ 500,000	$ 0	$ 0
Good Will	$ 0	$ 2,000,000	$ 2,000,000[1]	$ 700,000
	$3,000,000	$10,000,000	$ 7,000,000	$1,850,000

[1] indicates an asset whose gain is taxed as ordinary income
[2] indicates an asset whose gain is taxed as a capital gain.

The effective tax rate on the sales proceeds is 18.5% ($1,850,000 tax liability divided by the $10,000,000 sales proceeds). The effective tax rate on the "taxable gain" is 26% ($1,850,000 tax liability divided by the $7,000,000 taxable gain).

If you receive an offer from an Outsider to purchase your company, you should ask your accountant to calculate the taxes that will be due on your sales proceeds and the after-tax amount you will be able to "bank" after the sale. You might want to compare the net after-tax proceeds you will receive from a sale to an Outsider versus the amount you will receive from a sale to an ESOP.

When an owner sells to an ESOP, he or she almost always sells stock (more than 99% of the time). If the company is an S corporation at the time of the sale, the owner will pay tax at capital gains tax rates. If the company is a C corporation, the owner may be able to defer tax, perhaps even permanently (See Chapter 10 Q&As 12 and 32). In either event, a sale to an ESOP will, in most situations, result in substantial tax savings for the selling shareholders.

Maximize Price

Many of the business owners with whom I speak assume that they will be paid more if they sell to an Outsider than if they sell to an ESOP. In most cases, this is not true.

In general, there are two types of buyers: financial buyers and strategic buyers.

A financial buyer purchases a company for its future cash flow and pays the seller a multiple of cash flow based upon prevailing market conditions. For example, a financial buyer, such as a private equity group (PEG) or a private investor may pay five times the company's expected future cash flow, generally defined as Earning Before Interest Taxes Depreciation and Amortization (EBITDA). An ESOP is not allowed to pay more than the maximum amount a financial buyer would pay but an ESOP can pay as much as any other financial buyer.

A strategic buyer, such as a competitor or supplier, may pay more than a financial buyer because of potential cost savings, new revenue opportunities and other synergies. Business owners may receive a higher price from a strategic buyer than they could receive from an ESOP or other financial buyer.

Therefore, it is not entirely true that an ESOP cannot pay as much as other buyers. An ESOP can pay as much as other financial buyers, which may be less than what a strategic buyer would pay.

TILL DEATH DO US PART

Some business owners say they want to "die with their boots on." Often these individuals have their work and much of their identity and self-worth tied to their involvement with their company. It's not unusual to see these business owners work well into their 70's.

There are several risks inherent in a "till death do us part" strategy.

During the economic turmoil that engulfed the world beginning in the later part of 2007, many business owners who had been highly successful for decades saw their companies suffer a dramatic downturn or even fail. Companies involved in manufacturing and construction were particularly hard hit.

Consider a 70-year-old business owner who in July 2007 had a construction or manufacturing company worth $10 million, 401k and personal investments worth $2 million and a home and personal property worth $1 million. Eighteen months later his home and 401k could have dropped in value 20-40% and his construction or manufacturing company could have been liquidated with the proceeds used to pay off its debts.

Most of us know someone who experienced this type of financial melt down. The lesson to be learned is that diversification and asset allocation are critical to protecting our financial security. What would have happened to this business owner if he had sold 50 percent of his company to an ESOP for $5 million prior to the economic downturn and invested that money very conservatively? He would have lost some of his net worth as a result of the recession, but he would have been much more financially secure. Selling to an ESOP would have enabled him to have enhanced his financial security while allowing him to continue to work for and to control his company for as long as he chose to do so.

Another risk inherent in a "till death do us part" strategy is the risk of disability or pre-mature death. In many small to mid-size companies, if the owner becomes disabled or dies, the company may have to be sold for a fraction of its value. Owners can protect themselves from this risk with buy-sell agreements and with disability and life insurance, but ESOPs also can play a valuable role. (See the case study in Chapter 6).

The final risk I will discuss inherent in a "till death do us part" strategy is the potential loss of key employees. Here's a common situation: A company with a single owner who is age 55 has a 30-year-old key employee who the owner thinks will be able to run the company after he is gone. Here's the dilemma: If the owner plans to work his entire life, how can he keep the key employee "engaged" for the next 20 years?

As you undoubtedly know, we entrepreneurs are impatient by nature.

Therefore, a young key employee who truly will be able to run your company some day likely will not be satisfied with your telling him that he can purchase your company from your estate after you die. Any successor who is worth having is going to be too impatient to accept this type of amorphous planning. Instead, the successor is going to want to see a more concrete planning structure in place and he is going to want to have some significant role and decision-making authority before the time he is 55. In our example, the key employee is 30 and the owner's life expectancy is 25 years.

CONCLUSION

When it comes to Succession Planning, there is no single strategy that works best in every situation. My goal in elaborating on some of the problems inherent in the three traditional strategies (Sell to an Insider, Sell to an Outsider and "Till Death Do Us Part") is not to discourage you from employing one of them. Rather, my point is to provide an honest and balanced comparison of the advantages and disadvantages of these traditional strategies compared to an ESOP. My hope is that you will work with your advisors and a knowledgeable ESOP consultant to select the strategy that works best for you. In the next Chapter, I provide a questionnaire you can use to help begin the process of selecting the succession planning strategy that will work best for you.

3

SELECTING AN OWNERSHIP SUCCESSION PLANNING STRATEGY

*N*ow that you know what an ESOP is and how it works (Chapter 1) and how an ESOP compares to other Succession Planning strategies (Chapter 2), the next step is for you to determine which Succession Planning option is best based upon your unique situation and goals.

Historically, many advisors have counseled business owners by describing their planning options and the pros and cons of each option. While this is a good start, it doesn't go far enough. Owners often get lost in a morass of technical detail and are no closer to making a decision than when they began.

We have found that a more directive approach to counseling business owners often is more productive. This directive approach uses our copyrighted Ownership Succession Planning Assessment. The Assessment is a series of questions that lead a business owner to a decision by narrowing the field of potential solutions until there is only one solution left standing.

This type of Assessment is not a new concept; it is frequently used by management consultants in advising Fortune 500 companies. We have found that it also works well in advising business owners on Ownership Succession Planning.

Our Ownership Succession Planning Assessment should be used as part of a planning process that involves your accountant, attorney, financial advisor and banker.

The Assessment begins with the premise that there are four potential Ownership Succession Planning Strategies:
- Sell to an Outsider
- Sell to an Insider
- Till death do us part
- Employee Stock Ownership Plan (ESOP)

The Assessment asks questions related to each of these options.

The first series of questions is designed to help you determine if you are a good candidate to sell to an Outsider.

In each pair of statements, choose the one that best describes your thoughts.

1. ☐ I would like to sell my company to an outsider, take the money and run.
   ☐ I would like for key employees and/or children to have the company.

2. ☐ I am burned out with my company and want to separate myself from it.
   ☐ I want to stay involved in my company (but perhaps less active in day-to-day operations) and its continuing success will be part of my legacy.

3. ☐ I would like to do something entirely different in the next phase of my life.
   ☐ I would like to transition gradually from my current role as the operator of my company to a new role as a mentor.

If you chose the first statement in at least two of these pairs, you may be a good candidate to sell to an Outsider. Speak with someone who could help you orchestrate a sale to an Outsider. For example, ask your current advisors to introduce you to a business broker or an investment banker. Business brokers generally are appropriate for transactions of less than $5 million and investment bankers for transactions of $5 million plus. Fees for investment bankers and business brokers generally are calculated as a percentage of the sale price. You may want to meet with at least two investment bankers or business brokers to find someone who you feel you can work well with and to make sure you are getting a reasonable fee.

If you chose the first statement in at least two of the pairs, you are finished with the Assessment. If you chose the second statement in at least two of the pairs, you should proceed to the next series.

4. ☐ Work is my life and I don't ever want to slow down.
    ☐ I want to stay involved in my company but perhaps less active in day-to-day operations.

5. ☐ The company could not succeed without me and I don't currently have a successor in place.
    ☐ My successors (key employees or children) could run the company today or could be prepared to do so in 24 months.

6. ☐ I am in excellent-to-good health and have plenty of energy and stamina.
    ☐ I am in poor health and do not have nearly the energy I had a few years ago.

If you chose the first statement in at least two of the pairs, you may be a good candidate for a "Till death do us part" strategy. Discuss estate and gift tax planning with your attorney and estate liquidity and risk management with your financial advisor. You also may want to discuss how you could create a retention plan for your potential successors. Consider strategies such as an insured buy-sell agreement and an equity-based incentive program such as a Stock Appreciation Rights or Phantom Stock Plan.

If you chose the first statement in two or more pairs, you are finished with the Assessment. If you chose the second statement in two or more of the pairs, proceed to the next series of questions. Circle one for each.

7. **Yes or No**   I and/or my Company pay tax at the highest rate.
8. **Yes or No**   I need some upfront cash in addition to some annual income from my Company.
9. **Yes or No**   I have children I want to succeed me in the Company but I also have children who won't be involved.
10. **Yes or No**   I would like my employees to have a financial incentive to focus on the Company's long-term profitability.

If you answered "Yes" to at least two of these four questions, you should consider an ESOP as your sole succession planning strategy or the use of an ESOP in conjunction with a sale to an Insider or a "Till death do us part" strategy.

There are a number of key points involved in this Assessment. The first is that selecting a planning strategy does not have to be an all-or-nothing proposition. A partial sale to an ESOP today does not preclude a future sale to an Outsider. An ESOP can work well in conjunction with a sale to an Insider or a "Till death do us part" approach.

The second key point is that an ESOP should always be considered when the goal is a transfer to Insiders. As explained in Chapter 2, an ESOP offers compelling tax benefits on transfers to Insiders. Transfers to Insiders can usually be made more cost effective by using an ESOP.

The final key point to consider is that in certain situations when an owner thinks he wants to sell to an Outsider, he ends up selling to an ESOP instead. In Chapter 2, we discussed some of the provisions purchasers want included in sales agreements – indemnifications, escrows, employment agreements, and earn-outs. On more than one occasion, we have had clients terminate negotiations on a sale to an Outsider because the Outsider pushed too aggressively on some of these points of negotiation. The potential sellers had the ESOP as a fall-back purchaser and sold to it instead of an Outsider.

I hope that this Assessment is helpful in your planning process. Remember, use it in conjunction with, not in lieu of, your advisors. And if you're ready for an ESOP coach, you can contact us. We can talk with you about how an ESOP could work to help achieve your goals.

4

EASY AS PI/PIE

*M*any of the ESOPs I have worked on over the past 25-plus years have been about as "easy as pi." For those of you who, like me, slept through algebra class, here is how Wikipedia defines "pi."

"Pi is a mathematical constant whose value is the ratio of any circle's circumference to its diameter in Euclidean space; this is the same value as the ratio of a circle's area to the square of its radius."

If you have no idea what that means, welcome to the club. Unfortunately, some ESOPs are about as difficult to understand and implement as pi. However, there are some that are relatively simple and straightforward – as "easy as pie." The first case study I will share is about one of the easiest, most pleasant ESOP experiences I've ever had.

The story begins with my client being invited to the headquarters of one of his competitors. The competitor was interested in purchasing my client's Company and during this meeting offered to pay $25 million for the Company. The CEO of the target company asked the potential purchaser about the terms of the purchase. When the purchaser said "cash at closing," my client was shocked. The purchaser wasn't much bigger than my client. My client asked how they were going to be able to borrow $25 million to purchase his Company. What the purchaser said intrigued my client.

The would-be purchaser said that several years ago their company had become a 100% ESOP-owned S corporation. As a result, the company operated as a tax-free entity. Neither the company nor its shareholders paid tax on the company's earnings. The potential purchaser had "banked" its tax savings and had created a "war chest" that it could use to make acquisitions.

My client's CEO politely thanked the potential purchaser, said he would consider the offer and get back to him with a decision. However, on the plane ride home, the CEO declared that they were not going to sell to the competitor. Instead they were going to do what their competitor had done. They were going to become a 100% ESOP-owned S corporation.

The next week, I got a call from the Company's CFO. He said that a few years prior he had attended a seminar at which I had spoken on ESOPs. He had kept the handout materials with my name and phone number and said that he would like to meet to discuss their situation.

There are a couple of reasons I consider this ESOP experience "easy as pie." The first is that the executives who run this Company are some of the nicest, smartest and most competent business owners with whom I've ever had the pleasure to work. The second reason is that all of the numbers just fell into place, as I explain below.

The three owners would be selling their S corporation stock to the ESOP for $25 million. (*Note that this is the same amount the competitor had offered.*) The annual debt service on the ESOP loan would be $4.5 million. The next chart illustrates how the Company would come up with the $4.5 million per year it would need to service the ESOP debt.

	Pre-ESOP	Post-ESOP	Savings
Shareholder Comp	$ 4,045,296	$ 800,000	$ 3,245,296
Rent to Related Parties	$ 1,164,677	$ 679,710	$ 484,967
401 Match	$ 147,000	$ 0	$ 147,000
Miscellaneous	$ 216,000	$ 0	$ 216,000
			$ 4,093,263

The "shareholder comp" line shows that the total compensation of the Company's two top shareholders before the ESOP ("pre") was $4,045,296.

One of the shareholders was age 64 and would be retiring coincident with the establishment of the ESOP. The other major shareholder (age 52) would be reducing his base salary to $400,000 per year and would have the potential to earn an additional $400,000 in bonuses and long-term incentive payments if the Company hit its financial targets each year after the ESOP was established. This "shareholder comp" line assumes the maximum annual payment to the shareholder.

Prior to establishing the ESOP, the Company matched employee 401k contributions dollar for dollar capped at $750. When it established the ESOP, the Company suspended its 401k contribution, saving the Company $147,000 per year. (More on this later in the case study).

The Company had other miscellaneous cost savings totaling $216,000. This included items such as "excess" travel and entertainment, "excess" club dues and related expenses.

As I said above, one of the reasons this case was so easy is that "all the numbers just fell into place." What I meant by that should now be obvious: The cost savings associated with the ESOP ($4 million) paid 88% of the ESOP's annual debt service of $4.5 million. This left the Company with an incremental cost to do the ESOP of $500,000, which was just over 11% of the Company's pre-tax income. Therefore, this Company was able to do an ESOP without it having a meaningful impact on the Company's profitability or cash flow.

Let's get back to one of the points I mentioned earlier. I said that when the company established the ESOP, it suspended its contribution to its 401k plan, a very common practice. However, as explained later, the Company contribution to the ESOP will be $1.25 million per year, nearly 10-times more than its 401k contribution.

Since the Company wanted to continue to provide a strong incentive for its employees to contribute to the 401k on a pre-tax basis, the Company used a portion of its annual contribution to the ESOP as a match on employee contributions to the 401k. The 401k plan was amended to state that employee contributions to the 401k plan would be matched with contributions to the ESOP. The matching formula would be: Every

$1 of cash employees contribute to their 401k will be matched with a $1 contribution of stock to their ESOP account. This is the same contribution formula that was in place before the ESOP but there are two important differences.

First, there is no cap on the ESOP match – there had been a cap of $750 on the 401k match. Second, the 401k match cost the Company $140,000 per year of cash. The stock match in the ESOP produced no Company cash cost. The Company would be contributing $1.25 million to the ESOP to service the ESOP Inside loan each year. This would result in the same amount being contributed (or allocated) to participant accounts. The only question would be how the $1.25 million would be divided among the participants. In this case the ESOP Trustee first used a portion of the $1.25 million as a match on employee 401k deferrals. The remainder would then be divided among the employees on a "salary ratio" basis. The next two charts illustrate these points.

SALARY RATIO ALLOCATION

$$\frac{\text{Sample Employee's W-2} \quad \$ \quad 30{,}000}{\text{Total Co W-2's} \quad \$18{,}000{,}000} = .16\%$$

In the above example of a salary ratio allocation calculation, we assume a sample employee with wages of $30,000, which equal .16% of the Company's total wages ($18 million). Therefore, this employee is entitled to a salary ratio contribution of .16% of the $970,000 value of shares available for allocation after the match. This will result in this employee receiving a salary ratio allocation of $1,552. (Please note that for illustrative purposes we have rounded numbers. This would not be done in the plan administration process.)

Assuming this employee contributes 4% of his pay to the 401k, his total Company paid retirement contribution for this year would be $2,752, calculated as follows.

$$\begin{array}{lcl}
\text{Employee 401k Contribution} & = & \$1,200 \\
\text{Company Match @ \$1 per \$1} & = & \$1,200 \\
\text{ESOP Salary Ratio Contribution} & = & \$1,552
\end{array}$$

This employee's total retirement plan contribution for the year will be $3,952. He will contribute $1,200 and the Company will contribute $2,752.

Many ESOP advisors focus only on the benefits ESOPs provide to selling shareholders and to the companies that sponsor the plans. However, as can be seen from this case study, ESOPs also provide very generous retirement benefits for the sponsoring company's employees. The next chart compares a typical rank-and-file employee's annual retirement plan contributions before and after the Company established an ESOP.

Pre-ESOP		Post-ESOP
$ 750	Employee 401k Contribution	$1,200
$ 750	Company Match	$1,200
$ 0	ESOP Contribution	$1,552
$1,500	Total Retirement Savings	$3,952
5%	Savings as % of Pay	13%

Prior to the ESOP, this employee contributed $750 to the 401k plan so that he could receive the maximum company matching contribution. After the ESOP was established and the $750 cap on the Company match was eliminated, the employee contributed 4% of his pay ($1,200) to the 401k Plan. It was matched with a $1,200 stock contribution to his ESOP account. Many of this Company's employees increased their 401k contributions which resulted in the Company matching contribution doubling from $140,000 to $280,000 per year.

The results for this Company's employees are typical for ESOP companies. Non-ESOP companies, on average, contribute 4% of employee pay to the company's retirement plan. ESOP companies, on average, contribute 10% of employee pay to the company's retirement plan. This is why we say that ESOPs benefit all of their constituencies, including the sponsoring company's employees.

One final point on this case study: In Chapter 1, I stated that many times the terms of the Inside Loan (between the company and the ESOP) are identical to the terms of the Outside Loan (between the bank and the company). This Case Study illustrates a situation where there was a difference between the loans.

The terms of the Outside Loans were as follows:

Outside Loan	$25,000,000	
– Bank Loan	$15,000,000	5 years
– Seller Notes	$10,000,000	Years 1-5 interest only
		Years 6-10 principal & interest

The Outside Loan was structured so that it would be fully paid over 10 years. The Selling Shareholders received $15 million the day the sale to the ESOP was closed. They received interest on their Seller Notes while the bank loan was being repaid and received payments of principal and interest in years 6-10.

The Inside Loan repayment was 20 years, twice as long as the Outside Loan. The reason for this mismatch is that the Inside Loan determines the number of shares that will be allocated (contributed to employees' ESOP accounts) each year. In this particular case, paying off the Inside Loan over 10 years would have resulted in employees receiving an ESOP contribution equal to 18% of their pay. By stretching the Inside Loan over 20 years, employees received an ESOP contribution of 9% per year. While this Company wanted to make a generous retirement plan contribution for its employees (9% is more than twice the national average company contribution to a retirement plan), it felt that an 18% contribution was excessive.

The chart below illustrates the annual cash flow to service the mismatched Inside/Outside Loan for this particular Company. For the sake of simplicity, I have used round numbers.

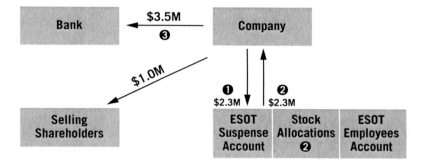

In Step 1, the Company makes a cash contribution of $2.3 million to the ESOP trust (ESOT). In Step 2, the ESOP uses that cash to make a payment on the Inside Loan of $2.3 million. This payment consists of principal and interest on the loan. This Inside Loan payment results in a release of shares from the ESOT's suspense account. Since the Inside Loan is for a period greater than 10 years, the "principal and interest" method for calculating share release must be used (see Chapter 9, Q&A 26). This results in 5% of the shares being released from the Suspense Account and those shares being allocated to participants' accounts. The value at which those shares are released is the price the ESOP paid for the shares – in this case $25 million. This results in shares having a value of $1.25 million being allocated to participants' accounts.

The following illustrates the calculation in determining the shares released from the ESOT Suspense Account using the Principal and Interest method. For further explanation see Chapter 9 Q&As 24-28.

Total P&I Over Life of Loan	$46,000,000
This Year P&I Payment	$2,300,000
Shares Released	.05 (5%)

In Step 3, the Company pays the amount due under the Outside Loans to the Outside Lenders – the bank and the Selling Shareholders.

As you will note, the $2.3 million annual contribution to the ESOP and payment on the Inside Loan is just over 50% of the amount due in annual payments on the Outside Loan ($4.5 million). If this Company had not become a 100% ESOP-owned S corporation, this could have been a problem. The problem would result from the fact that the Company would only get a tax deduction of $2.3 million (the payment on the Inside Loan), while it had a total annual ESOP cost of $4.5 million. However, as a 100% ESOP-owned S corporation, the mismatch of cash flow and tax benefits was immaterial since the Company will operate as a tax-exempt entity.

5

ALL IN THE FAMILY

*T*his case study is about a family-owned business located in a small town. The Company is owned and run by a husband and wife who are in their early 60's, with the help of their son. Their daughter lives in another city and has no interest in being involved in the Company.

We were referred to this Company by their investment advisor. We had structured an ESOP for the investment advisor's firm and he was so pleased with the results that he introduced us to several of his clients.

The owners of this Company had these objectives:

- They wanted to ensure that they would be financially secure when they retired. The Company was valued at $10 million. They had accumulated $3 million in investable assets outside the Company and their investment advisor told them that if they could get $5 million out of their Company, they would be able to live off the investment income generated by their $8 million portfolio.

- They wanted to structure their estate plan so that each child would receive 50% of their estate. However, they didn't want their daughter to get any of the Company stock since she wasn't active in the business.

- They wanted to minimize the impact of taxes on their financial and estate planning.

I have found that when working with family-owned businesses, one of their greatest challenges is what is referred to as "estate equalization." Parents generally want to leave equal portions of their estate to each of their children. However, this can be difficult to accomplish when the value of the business is the estate's largest asset and when you have children who are active in the business and children who are inactive. For example, in this case if the parents left the active son the business ($10 million) and the inactive daughter their investment portfolio ($3 million), the children would not be treated equally.

It is almost never a good idea to leave company stock to inactive children since this generally creates a conflict. ("He hit me first…") The inactive children want cash distributions from the business despite the fact that they don't work there. The active children want to be paid the maximum amount possible for their efforts and want to leave some cash in the business for future capital expenditures. This conflict of interests often results in family strife.

An ESOP can help solve this problem. Here is how it helped solve it in this particular case.

The parents sold 51% of their stock to the ESOP for $5.1 million. Since their Company was a C corporation, they were able to invest their ESOP sales proceeds in "qualified replacement property" (QRP) without paying tax on the proceeds. They turned the management of this money over to their investment advisor who created a portfolio of high grade corporate bonds which qualified as QRP (see Chapter 10, Q&As 10-26). The income generated by this bond portfolio plus the income generated by their other assets produced a nice retirement income.

At their death, their inactive child will receive the $5.1 million bond portfolio. She will be able to liquidate the portfolio without paying income tax due to the step-up in basis rules (see Chapter 10, Q&A 4). Immediately after the ESOP was implemented, the parents gifted their 49% interest in the Company to their son. However, the value of this gift for gift tax purposes was substantially less than what you might expect, as explained below.

If the Company is worth $10 million and the parents sell 51% of their stock to the ESOP for $5.1 million, you might well assume that the stock they've retained would be valued at $4.9 million. While that seems logical, the result actually is much better from a gift tax valuation perspective, which will result in substantial gift tax savings.

Prior to the ESOP, the value of the Company was $10 million. This represents the value of the Company's equity, net of its debt. For example, if the value of the Company was $12 million and it had $2 million in debt, the net value of the Company for purposes of a sale would be $10 million.

As a result of the ESOP transaction, the Company had taken on $5.1 million of new debt used to finance the ESOP's stock purchase. This reduced the net value of the Company from $10 million (pre-ESOP) to $4.9 million (post-ESOP). This results in the parents' 49% interest being valued at $2.4 million net of the debt (49% of $4.9 million).

The other valuation consideration that comes into play is the "minority interest discount" (see Chapter 12, Q&As 10-14). The concept behind the minority interest discount is that a controlling interest is worth more than a non-controlling interest. If I own a controlling interest in a company, I can make most corporate decisions without the approval of the non-controlling owners. Therefore, 51% of a $10 million company is worth $5.1 million and 49% is worth less than $4.9 million. In general, minority interest discounts range from 20-40%. In this case we've assumed a minority interest discount of 20% which will result in a gift of 49% of this Company's stock having a gift tax value of $1.92 million ($2.4 million – 20% minority interest discount).

The chart below shows the gift tax valuation concepts involved in this strategy.

49% of Company without ESOP Debt	$4.9 million
49% of Company after ESOP Debt	$2.4 million
Gift of a non-controlling 49% Interest (20% minority interest discount)	$1.92 million

We discussed with this client the potential of the parents making the stock gift to a family limited partnership rather than making it directly to their active child. This could have produced additional valuation discounts for "lack of marketability" (see Chapter 12, Q&A 15). However, this client decided that the elimination of tax on their sales proceeds (via 1042 QRP investments) and the 60% gift tax valuation reduction produced adequate tax savings.

There were two interesting planning challenges involved in this case.

Challenge 1: The first challenge had to do with the requirements of the Section 1042 tax-favored treatment of the sales proceeds. One of the rules involved with Section 1042 is referred to as the "Prohibited Allocation" rule (see Chapter 10, Q&As 27-31). This rule prohibited the active son from participating in the ESOP. As a result, he would not have an ESOP account.

We dealt with this planning challenge by having the Company create a Stock Appreciation Rights plan (SAR) for the active son. Under this Plan, the son would receive contributions to a deferred compensation plan account equal to the value of the stock that would have been contributed to his ESOP account. The value of this account will grow at the same rate that the ESOP shares grow. As a result, the son will receive the same value he would have received under the ESOP. Problem solved.

Challenge 2: The second challenge had to do with the need to sell 51% of the stock to the ESOP in order to take advantage of the minority interest discount when the parents gave their remaining stock to the active son. Often in planning with family-owned companies, the parents want to insure that their child(ren) will have a controlling interest in the company.

This challenge will be resolved as a result of the passage of time. As ESOP participants become entitled to distributions as a result of their death, disability or retirement, the Company will purchase the shares in their ESOP accounts. In relatively short order, this process will result in the son's shares constituting a majority of the outstanding shares as explained below.

Here's how it all looks in reality. Assume that the parents owned 1,000 shares (100%) of the Company's stock. They sell 51% (510 shares) to the ESOP. They gift their remaining 490 shares to the son.

During the first few years of the ESOP's existence, several employee participants quit. The Company purchases the vested shares from their account, cash is distributed to participants and stock purchased by the Company is retired. Assuming that 30 shares are purchased by the Company through this process (known as a stock redemption), there will be 970 shares outstanding. The 30 shares that were redeemed will be retired as treasury stock. Now that there are 970 shares outstanding, the Company's ownership breakdown is as follows.

ESOP   480 shares (49%)
Son   490 shares (51%)

As a result of this redemption/distribution process, the son will own a majority of the stock in a very short period of time. Over the next 20 years, the son could end-up owning 80-plus percent of the Company through this process.

As can be seen, ESOPs can work well in family-owned companies and can help solve some of the challenges that often exist in planning for their succession.

6

NEITHER A BORROWER NOR A LENDER BE

November of 2007 was a time of great economic uncertainty. Lehman Brothers had collapsed. There was a meltdown in the credit markets as a result of the subprime debacle. We were in the midst of the second-worst stock market in history. This might not seem like the best time for a business owner to begin a business succession planning project, especially if the company is in the contracting/construction business. But that is exactly what one company did.

This client was referred to us by his CPA, Don. Don and I had known each other for 20 years and had a number of mutual clients.

The Company was owned by a gentleman in his early 70's. He had three long-term key employees who were his anointed successors. He had begun his succession planning several years ago when the Company purchased $2 million of life insurance to fund a buy-sell agreement with the successors. However, the Company was now worth $4 million and the owner was uninsurable.

The Company wanted to use an ESOP to fill the gap between the Company's value ($4 million) and the amount of life insurance funding that was in place ($2 million).

Our first thought was that the Company should implement a leveraged ESOP. Under this structure the Company would borrow money to fund the ESOP's purchase of $2 million of stock from the owner. The loan could come from the Company's bank, from a Seller Note or from a combination of these two sources. However, because of the credit market meltdown, it was virtually impossible to get a loan during November 2007. Therefore, we suggested that the owner consider funding the entire sale with Seller Notes. We had many clients who had used this approach during the credit crunch. It gave them the ability to implement a plan without being dependent on bank credit.

While Seller Note financing was more attractive to this business owner than bank financing, he wanted to take a super-conservative approach that would eliminate the need for any debt. After all, even if he were the "bank," the Company would be increasing its debt during a time of great economic uncertainty. To a conservative business owner, this didn't seem like a prudent decision.

The plan we implemented was an "unleveraged" ESOP, meaning that there was no debt. Under this approach, the Company would evaluate its financial situation at the end of each year and determine how much, if any, stock it would have the ESOP purchase from the owner. At the end of 2007, the Company had a profit of $500,000, which it contributed to the ESOP. The ESOP used this money to purchase $500,000 of stock from the owner.

There are several key points to keep in mind when considering an unleveraged ESOP.

Value of the stock to be purchased

When selling to a leveraged ESOP, an owner sells a block of stock for a price established pursuant to an independent professional valuation (see Chapter 12). The price of the stock is established as of the date of sale. Any increases or decreases in value following the sale will have no impact on the seller. In this example, the owner would have sold half of his stock for $2 million.

With an unleveraged ESOP the price is determined in the same way. However, the price of future sales cannot be locked-in at today's value. Therefore, the business owner assumes the risk that the value of the stock may decrease in the future. If this Company had 1,000 shares issued and outstanding at a $4 million valuation, each share would be worth $4,000. Therefore, $500,000 would purchase 125 shares. However, if the Company's value decreased the next year by 15%, each share would be worth $3,400 and $500,000 would purchase 147 shares. Please note that for the sake of keeping this example as simple as possible we have ignored minority interest discounts used in valuations.

The point is that an ESOP cannot enter into an agreement to purchase stock in the future at a predetermined price. The ESOP cannot pay more than fair market value of the stock determined "as of the date of the sale" by an independent professional appraiser/valuation consultant. Therefore, when using an unleveraged ESOP, the owner assumes the risk of future fluctuations in stock price. Of course, if the price the ESOP can pay for stock at some point in the future is not acceptable to the owner, he doesn't have to sell. It also should be noted that if a company's value is increasing, it could benefit an owner to do an unleveraged ESOP and to reap the benefit of future stock appreciation.

Allocation of stock to participants' accounts

With a leveraged ESOP, shares that are purchased are initially held in the ESOP "suspense account" and are allocated to participants as the ESOP debt is repaid (see Chapter 9 Q&As 24-28). In contrast, with an unleveraged ESOP, there is no ESOP suspense account and all shares are allocated to participants' accounts immediately upon being purchased.

Consider the following example that illustrates the difference in share allocations between a leveraged and unleveraged ESOP. Assume that in each case we have 500 total shares to be purchased for $2 million. In the first example we'll assume that the 500 shares will be purchased by a leveraged ESOP, using a 7-year loan. In this case, shares will be released (using the principal only method of share release) in equal amounts over seven years resulting in 71.43 shares being released each year. If we had used an unleveraged ESOP and the Company had contributed $500,000 per year – assuming that the stock value didn't change – all of the shares would be purchased and allocated in four years. This would result in 125 shares being allocated to participants each year – a much faster share allocation than the leveraged ESOP.

The faster share allocation often is not an issue for business owners. However, it should be quantified and evaluated prior to implementing a plan.

Owner's income tax consequences. If the owner had taken the Company's $500,000 year-end profit as a bonus, his federal income tax liability would be $175,000 (35% of $500,000). However, if the Company contributes $500,000 to the ESOP, which it uses to purchase stock from the owner, his federal tax liability will be $75,000 (15% of $500,000). The owner saves $100,000 in taxes as a result of paying capital gains tax on sales proceeds as opposed to paying regular income tax on a bonus. The total tax savings on the full $2 million stock value would be $400,000.

We structure many more leveraged than unleveraged ESOPs. However, unleveraged ESOPs have an important role in business succession planning, especially during times of economic uncertainty and tight credit markets.

7

ULTIMATE ESOP SUCCESS

I have entitled this chapter "Ultimate ESOP Success" because I think it is the best representation I've seen of Louis Kelso's dream of ESOPs enabling more Americans to accumulate capital. (Louis Kelso was the investment banker and economist generally credited with creating ESOPs.) This is the story of how an ESOP ignited a serial entrepreneur and how the ESOP benefited his employees and literally thousands of charitable beneficiaries.

Jack, the business owner, grew up in a rural community. His parents instilled a work ethic and entrepreneurial courage that laid the foundation for his success.

In college he pursued an accounting degree, then worked in pharmaceutical sales and accounting. At the age of 25, Jack went to work as the controller of a company that managed seven nursing homes. Then, without warning, came a pivotal moment that would transform him from a businessman to a leader.

On a Friday evening, the entire staff of one of the nursing homes staged a walk-out, leaving 110 elderly patients uncared for. He gathered his wife (who had a bit of nursing training) and a couple of employees from the corporate staff and they began calling people to ask for help. They managed somehow to pull in enough people to take care of the patients that weekend.

The owner of the company was so impressed with Jack's work that he made him president of the company at age 27. Soon he was growing the company by making acquisitions and building new nursing homes. Within a year the company had doubled its facilities and become very profitable.

After two years in this position, Jack resigned and started his own company managing nursing homes. Within 10 years he managed 20 facilities employing over 3,000 people.

Twenty years in the nursing home business took its toll. Jack was burned out and ready to move on. He started looking for an exit strategy. He considered selling his company, but knew that would mean his corporate management staff would lose their jobs. He didn't like the idea of walking down the street of his small town a rich man and seeing employees who had been loyal to him for years now unemployed.

He was determined to find a better option; a way that would still allow him to get rich but without causing his employees to lose their jobs. Someone mentioned an ESOP as an exit strategy, and he was inspired. He spent a great deal of time researching ESOPs and decided it was the best way for him to achieve his goals.

He created an ESOP for his nursing home management company and sold the company to the ESOP for almost $50 million. He has now parlayed that into a net worth of several hundred million dollars.

The employees of the nursing homes have benefitted greatly from the ESOP. I have a family member who was able to take early retirement because of the large nest egg accumulated in her ESOP account. Almost all of the residents of the county in which Jack lives have benefitted from the wealth he created by starting the ESOP. He created a charitable foundation that provides scholarships to every high school graduate in the county. The scholarships can be used for a university, community college or technical school education. At this point, there are approximately 350 students in the program, which has an annual budget of $800,000.

Creating capital for employees was Louis Kelso's dream. ESOPs provide the tax incentives that encourage business owners to fulfill the dream.

ESOPs have the potential to benefit so many by providing capital for business owners, their employees and their communities.

ESOP COACH

8

ERISA REQUIREMENTS

*E*RISA, the law that governs retirement plans, is sometimes referred to by retirement plan professionals as: "Every Ridiculous Idea Since Adam." Actually ERISA stands for the Employee Retirement Income Security Act of 1974. However, for those of us who have had the experience of studying the minutia of ERISA, the former definition often seems more apt than the latter.

ERISA deals with the rules employers must comply with in order to reap the tax benefits of a "qualified" retirement plan. These employer tax benefits include tax deductible contributions and tax deferred growth of plan assets.

ERISA's rules are wide ranging and intricate. They deal with subjects such as:

- which employees must be covered by the Plan;
- how much the employer can contribute to the Plan, and
- when employees' accounts will become vested.

Failure to comply with these rules can result in dire consequences. However, by dealing with knowledgeable and experienced consultants and attorneys and by filing its Plan with the IRS for a "Favorable Determination Letter," an employer can rest assured that its Plan is structured properly.

It's not enough, however, for the Plan to be structured properly; it also must be operated consistent with ERISA and the Plan's provisions. This is best achieved by hiring a competent and experienced ESOP administrator. This is an area where I have seen employers make mistakes. Some employers attempt to administer their ESOP in-house. I have yet to meet a CFO or HR director with the ability to administer an ESOP. Another common mistake is for a company to assume that its 401k plan administrator can take care of its ESOP. ESOP accounting is very different from 401k and requires specialized knowledge and software. Hiring an ESOP administration specialist is well worth the small additional cost.

The Q&As that follow discuss some of ERISA's key requirements.

OVERVIEW

1. What is an ESOP?

An ESOP (employee stock ownership plan) is a qualified, defined contribution employee benefit plan that is required to invest primarily (generally over 50%) in the stock of the employer.

PARTICIPATION RULES

2. Who must be included in the ESOP? What are the minimum ESOP participation rules?

The rules for participation in an ESOP are the same as for other qualified retirement plans (pensions, profit sharing, etc.). The rules provide several tests to assure plans meet minimum anti-discrimination requirements. Virtually all ESOP companies, however, cover at least all employees who are 21 years of age or older, have at least one year of service and have at least 1,000 hours of service or more in a year. Employees covered by a collective bargaining agreement can be excluded from coverage, provided the company bargains in good faith about all retirement benefits. These are minimum requirements; companies can include more employees (such as part-time people or more recent hires).

The law does provide some additional exceptions. For instance, the ESOP can be set up to include only employees in a separate line of business within a company, such as a division or subsidiary, that has 50 or more employees. This will not apply, however, if the intent is to get around the coverage rules. For instance, a plan could not just cover a division set up of management people and exclude a division that just has non-management employees.

An alternative approach provides three tests for coverage. To use this approach, a company applies percentage tests to at least a minimum employee group. This group must include all employees 21 or older who have completed at least 1,000 hours of service in a plan year, but can exclude non-resident aliens, employees in a separate line of business with 50 or more employees and employees covered by a collective bargaining agreement. Except for these categories, for plan years starting on or before December 31, 1996, a plan must include the lesser of 50 employees or 40% of all employees. This requirement does not apply to plan years starting after December 31, 1996. After the exceptions have been taken, the tests can be met if:

1. At least 70% of non-highly compensated employees are covered,
2. The percentage of non-highly compensated employees who are covered is at least 70% of the percentage of highly compensated covered, or
3. There is a classification system that does not discriminate in favor of highly compensated employees and the average benefit percentage (generally, the percentage contributed to the plan) for the covered non-highly compensated group is at least 70% of that contributed to the covered highly compensated group.

Although these alternative tests are available, they are very, very rarely used in ESOPs. The kind of exclusion the rules provide is both contrary to the spirit most ESOP companies are trying to set up and may cause practical problems. Most importantly, if the eligible payroll base drops too low, the company may not have enough eligible payroll against which to make contributions and/or annual additions.

3. When must participation begin in an ESOP once an employee becomes eligible?

An employee who has satisfied the plan's minimum age and service requirements must begin participation in the plan not later than the first of (a) the first day of the plan year beginning after the date on which the requirements were met or (b) the date six months after the date on which the requirements are met. Participation can begin at an earlier date, however.

4. Aside from legal issues, what practical considerations should be taken into account in designing ESOP participation rules?

While the law permits various ways to narrow the participant base in an ESOP, there is a good reason ESOP companies want to use broad coverage rules: the ability to deduct contributions is limited to a percentage of eligible payroll. To the extent people are excluded, their payroll does not count. This can cause problems when an ESOP is being used to acquire a substantial amount of stock. Companies also need to consider whether limiting ownership will make it harder to create an ownership culture.

On the other side, union employees may be covered by agreements that provide them benefit plans that are different from employees not covered by a collective bargaining agreement. The union may be reluctant to change any of these in return for an ESOP; the company may be unwilling or unable to add the ESOP on top of existing benefits. In multi-unit companies, moreover, an ESOP may be practical for one business division but not for another. The law allows an ESOP to be limited in this way, given the caveats above, and usually allows the business unit to offer either stock in the parent company or itself.

5. Can an ESOP include employees working for the company as independent contractors ("1099 employees")?

No.

6. What about leased employees? Must or can they be included in the ESOP or 401k plan?

We will look first at the issue of whether you must cover them. The law requires these employees to be covered by your benefit plans if they are deemed to be "common law" employees. This basically is any leased employee working for you on a full-time basis who is under your control doing work done by people who normally work for you. Exceptions to this would be if leased employees constitute under 20% of the workforce, do not do work normally done by other employees, have worked under one year for the company or are covered by a money purchase pension plan operated by the leasing company that contributes at least 10% of pay per year. Leased or contract employees must work 1,500 hours in a year to be counted as full-time.

The rule is more nuanced if you want to count leased employees. To be covered, the employees either have to be substantially full-time (1,500 hours or 75% of what your common law employees in that job work) or your plan has to provide that part-time employees can be included in the plan. You can count any 12-month period for this, not just the plan or calendar year. Hours as a direct employee can be added to hours as a leased employee. You can limit inclusion to employees who have worked for one year. A problem can arise is if they are also covered by a qualified plan from their employer. Then there has to be a determination of who the common law employer is, you or the leasing company. The employee cannot be covered by plans in both for the same work. It is technically possible for plans to be co-adopted, but this is a complex issue that requires expert legal advice.

7. Do employees who are members of controlled group companies participate in an ESOP?

Employees who are members of a controlled group of corporations (see Q&A 8) would be required to participate in the benefit plan under the same rules as employees of the parent corporation. Essentially, the law treats employees of a controlled group of corporations as employees of the parent corporation. Testing rules for the plan, therefore, apply to all employees of the parent and its control group corporations. If the employer owns a partnership, however, that is not considered a corporation and its employees would not be eligible for inclusion in the ESOP.

8. What constitutes a "control group" relationship?

There are two types of control groups: parent-subsidiary and brother-sister.

A parent-subsidiary control group exists where one or more chains of corporations are connected to a common parent with the parent owning at least 80% of the total combined voting power of all classes of stock or 80% of the value of all classes of stock (excluding stock of the parent). A "brother-sister" control group exists where, in two or more corporations, five or fewer persons, estates, or trusts own:

- at least 80% of the voting power of all classes entitled to vote, or
- at least 80% of the total value of all shares and more than 50% of the total combined voting power or stock value of each corporation, but counting only ownership that is identical in each organization (that is, they have to own more than 50% of each).

9. **If a partnership chooses to be taxed as a corporation, can it have an ESOP?**

It appears that it could, but the partnership would have to set up a subsidiary that had stock. A partnership interest would not be an employer security.

10. **Can a leasing company (also called a Professional Employer Organization, or PEO) have an ESOP for its employees?**

A PEO employee working for a client organization (CO) (a "worksite employee") is often considered a common law employee of the CO, as when the worksite employee works full-time at the CO, is under the CO's control and does work normally done by the CO's employees. If a PEO's defined contribution plan (such as an ESOP) covers worksite employees who are common law employees of the CO where they work, the plan can be disqualified because it violates the exclusive benefit rule (which provides that the ESOP must be for the exclusive benefit of employees of the sponsoring company).

In Revenue Procedure 2002-21 (amplified in Revenue Procedure 2003-86), the IRS stated that to prevent disqualification, PEOs could either terminate their single-employer defined contribution plans or convert them to multiple employer plans. However, ESOPs cannot be multiple-employer plans, so it is doubtful whether a PEO can have an ESOP that covers worksite employees.

It appears that a PEO can have an ESOP covering only its back-office employees, but it is important to determine whether such a plan complies with the discrimination testing rules (see Q&A 2).

11. **Can a professional corporation have an ESOP?**

No, except in Minnesota, Virginia (except for medical practices and law firms), and North Carolina. In general, state laws prohibit anyone except a member of the profession from being an owner of a professional corporation and the ESOP trust is considered the owner of the ESOP's shares. In Minnesota, if the trustee of the ESOP is from the relevant profession, that qualifies the plan. In Virginia, the trustee must be from that profession, employees cannot receive stock distributions and non-professionals cannot get more than one-third the allocations in accounting firms and one-half in other firms.

12. How do employees own stock through an ESOP?

Each employee meeting eligibility requirements (generally full-time people with a year or more of service) participates in the plan and receives an allocation of stock each year. That allocation is subject to vesting. The employee actually gets the shares after leaving the company. Closely held companies must repurchase the shares or have the ESOP do it.

CONTRIBUTION LIMITS

13. What are the limits for the deductibility of contributions to ESOPs?

There are two limits to consider: the amount the company can contribute to the plan overall ("contribution limits") and the maximum annual addition to any one employee's account ("annual addition limits"). As long as contributions fall within these two limits, those contributions are fully deductible.

Annual Addition Limits

The annual addition limits are relatively simple and apply to all ESOPs: The maximum value a participant can receive in one year as an annual addition to his account is 100% of eligible pay or $49,000 (for plan years after 2008, indexed for inflation) whichever is less.

The one complication is for leveraged ESOPs: for them, the limit calculation does not use the current value of the assets added to the account. Instead, the limit applies to the value of the assets at the time they were purchased using the loan (this amount is equivalent to the value of the principal repaid). In other words, if the company's stock value is rising, the current value of the addition to a participant's account may exceed the annual addition limits above as long as the value of that addition calculated using the share price at the time of the transaction is under the limits. The IRS does also allow companies to use the current value of the shares released, but companies must choose to use the method in advance and use it on a consistent basis.

Contribution Limits

In a non-leveraged ESOP the company simply makes contributions of cash or stock to the plan. These contributions are limited to a maximum equal to 25% of the eligible pay of ESOP participants. This limit applies to both C and S corporations. If the company has other defined contribution plans, company (but not employee) contributions to these plans will reduce this limit dollar for dollar.

For leveraged ESOPs the limit on company contributions depends on whether the company is a C or S corporation.

In C corporations, the total company contribution limit is 25% of eligible pay to repay the principal each year. This limit is not reduced by contributions to other defined contribution plans. Interest payments and reallocated forfeitures do not count in any of the C corporation limitation calculations. Reasonable dividends on stock held in the ESOP are also deductible. "Reasonable" has not been specifically defined, but should not be much in excess of what similar companies might pay on similar earnings.

S corporation rules are more limiting. Interest payments and forfeitures do count toward the 25% of pay limitation. Distributions on shares can be used to go above the limits, but, as noted, are not tax deductible. Contributions to other defined contribution plans do reduce the maximum company contribution to the ESOP.

14. Can a company contribute more than 25% of covered payroll to an ESOP?

If the ESOP is leveraged and is in a C corporation, contributions to the ESOP count separately from other contributions to qualified plans, as well as to cash contributions made to the ESOP for reasons other than repaying the loan. So the 25% limit applies only to what is needed to repay the ESOP loan, not the aggregate of all contributions.

Otherwise, while excess contributions are technically allowed, it's not very practical. Contributions above the 25% of covered pay limit are not deductible and are subject to an excise tax that even a 100% S ESOP company would have to pay. The contributions might also result in allocations to the plan in excess of the annual addition limits, although this is less likely given the new limits set up in 2001.

15. What counts as eligible pay or eligible compensation to receive an ESOP allocation?

When calculating eligible pay, the limit is $245,000 in 2009, indexed for inflation after that in $5,000 increments. For plan years starting after December 31, 2001, any taxable pay can be included, plus 401k and cafeteria plan deferrals, although companies can define compensation more narrowly, such as straight pay, but not commissions, as long as this does not have the effect of discriminating against lower paid employees. Pay over $245,000 per year in 2009, to be indexed by inflation, is not eligible. Neither is the pay of anyone excluded because of the "1042" rules that prohibit the participation in the plan of sellers, their children, parents, siblings and spouses, as well as any 25% shareholders, in receiving ESOP allocations when the seller takes a tax deferral on sales to an ESOP.

In 2007, the IRS made some additional changes. The rules now provide that pre-tax elective deferrals under Code Sections 401k, 403(b), 457, 125, and 132(f)(4), as well as certain amounts for totally disabled participants under Section 22(e)(3), qualify as compensation. Generally, payments made after severance are excluded from compensation, but payments made within 2 ½ months after severance for accumulated sick leave, vacation or other paid time count, as well as payments that would have been paid absent severance for work outside normal working hours, commissions, bonuses, etc.

16. If someone is hired during the year and the ESOP's participation requirement is one year, come the following year will they be eligible to receive the ESOP contribution based on the full year's wages or just from the month they were hired to that month the next year?

It depends on the plan's entry dates. Say you have a calendar-year plan (January 1 to December 31), the employee is hired on September 1, 2008, and there is a one-year wait; however, the entry dates are only January 1 and July 1. In that case, the employee would not become a participant until January 1, 2010.

As for the compensation, that is also dependent on your plan. The plan can limit the compensation taken into account for allocation of contributions, but only from the time that a participant begins participation, not based on hire dates.

17. How much is enough to contribute to an ESOP? What is the typical amount contributed to an ESOP?

Employers often ask how much they should contribute to make the plan meaningful to employees. The average corporate contribution to all retirement-oriented plans combined is only about 4% of pay (this does not count employee contributions). The average ESOP contribution, according to various surveys, is about 6-10% of pay. Public companies tend to be at the lower range (a 1991 study by Michael Conte found they contribute an average of 6% of pay), while private companies are higher (8% in a 1994 Ohio study and 10% in a 1990 Michigan study). Over 80% of all ESOP participants also are in another company sponsored plan, often a 401k plan. How much is enough to make employees feel like owners, unfortunately, cannot be answered, but research does show the higher the contribution, the more employees feel like owners.

Whether calculating legal limits or practical guidelines, it is important to get qualified, ongoing advice. The penalties for violating the limits are severe but with planning are easily avoided.

18. Can contributions to an ESOP for a tax year be made after the end of that tax year?

Contributions for a given tax year can be made at any time up to the final due date for the company's tax return for that year, which can be as much as 8½ months after the end of the year if an extension is obtained. These contributions must be allocated based on compensation from the year for which the contribution is counted, however.

This applies, however, only if the plan is already set up in the tax year in question. Contributions to a plan set up in fiscal 2010, for instance, are not deductible for fiscal 2009 no matter when they are made. In addition, where there is an ESOP loan, the loan must have been in place by year end and shares must be deemed to have been released effective to the date the contribution is effective.

19. How do ESOP allocations interact with limits for other benefit plans?

The rules are as follows:

For plan years starting after December 31, 2001

Companies can make tax-deductible contributions of up to 25% of the aggregate eligible pay of employees in the plan (or plans), regardless of whether the ESOP is leveraged or whether it is in a C or S corporation. In C corporation ESOPs, reasonable dividends used to repay a loan, that are passed through to participants, or are reinvested by participants in company stock in the ESOP, do not count towards the 25% limit. Eligible pay is defined to include employee deferrals into 401k plans or cafeteria plans. This limit applies to the total amount of a company's contributions to its defined contribution plans (ESOPs, stock bonus plans, profit sharing plans and 401k plans). (See below in this answer for an exception for leveraged C corporation ESOPs.) Contributions to defined benefit plans do not count towards this limit. The maximum annual addition to any one individual's defined contribution accounts under the plans cannot exceed the lesser of 100% of pay or $49,000 in 2009, to be indexed for inflation thereafter in $1,000 increments. In C corporation ESOPs, dividends used to repay a loan, that are passed through to participants or are reinvested by participants in company stock in the ESOP, do not count toward the 100% of pay of maximum dollar limit. Employee deferrals do count toward the 100% of pay or maximum dollar limitation. Annual additions thus include all employer and employee contributions to defined contribution plans. In S corporations, interest payments and forfeitures count towards the maximum annual addition limits, and interest payments count towards the 25% of pay maximum deductible employer contribution.

The Impact of a Defined Benefit Plan

For plan years starting after December 31, 1999, defined benefit and defined contribution plan contributions do not have to be aggregated. Prior law required a complicated aggregation test.

Special Rules for Leveraged ESOPs

In C corporations only, leveraged ESOP sponsors are allowed to contribute and deduct up to 25% of eligible pay to cover principal payments on the ESOP debt. Interest is fully deductible. Aside from deduction limits, there is a separate limit on annual additions to employee accounts. In leveraged ESOPs in C corporations, interest and forfeitures do not count towards the limits for annual additions to employee accounts, but these special exceptions apply only if not more than one-third of the contributions are allocated to highly compensated people ("highly compensated" is defined by law and explained in the section "Highly Compensated Employees"). In addition, no one can get more than $49,000 in 2009 and 2010, a figure to be indexed for inflation in $1,000 increments annually. In a 2004 private letter ruling, the IRS concluded that this 25% of pay limit is, for an ESOP in a C corporation, in addition to contributions by the company to other qualified plans. If a company maintains another defined contribution plan, the contribution limits for each plan count separately. For instance, a company could contribute up to 50% of pay. This only applies to leveraged C corporation ESOPs, however.

In S corporations, interest payments and forfeitures do count toward the maximum individual allocation limits.

C corporations can go beyond the 25% limit, however, by paying "reasonable" dividends on the ESOP shares. These dividends are normally paid on all shares, allocated and unallocated. (Dividends can also be passed through directly to participants, but doing so does not raise the contribution limit because dividends are paid to employees, not the plan). "Reasonable" has never been legally defined, but most practitioners believe it means within the range paid on comparable classes of stock in similar companies, must be capable of being paid regularly, and must not result in unreasonable compensation. The dividends must be included in alternative minimum tax calculations.

20. When companies have multiple plans and a leveraged ESOP is one of them, does the 25% of pay limit apply to each or both together?

For plan years starting after December 31, 2001, the law provides that all forms of ESOPs can contribute up to 25% of eligible pay to the plan. The IRS ruled that contributions to an ESOP and other plans do not need to be aggregated for total eligible pay purposes in a leveraged C corporation ESOP, but this does not apply to other types of ESOPs.

If the ESOP is leveraged and is in a C corporation, contributions to the ESOP count separately from other contributions to qualified plans, so the 25% limit applies only to what is needed to repay the ESOP loan, not the aggregate of all contributions.

21. When companies have multiple plans, do allocation limit procedures have to be specified concerning which plan will have a reduction in contributions to meet the 415 rules?

Yes, it must be specified in each plan document.

22. For testing purposes, can contributions to another plan be used to offset contributions to an ESOP? For instance, can the fact that an employee is getting contributions under a separate profit sharing plan offset the requirement that the employee get a non-discriminatory contribution to the ESOP?

No. ESOP allocations generally cannot be offset by contributions to other plans. There is one exception:

1. Both plans were in effect November 1, 1977,
2. Both plans are ESOPs and the proportion of qualifying employer securities to total plan assets is substantially the same for both plans,
3. The plans each hold the same class of stock, and
4. If there is more than one class of stock held in the plans, the ratio of each class in each plan is substantially the same.

23. If an employee is on military leave, does that employee still get allocations of contributions to an ESOP for the time missed? How is the applicable pay rate for that time determined?

Under USERRA (the Uniformed Services Employment and Reemployment Rights Act), the law governing employer obligations to employees on military leave, if the employee returns to work after the service, he or she must be credited with allocations from the ESOP equal to what would have been received under the assumed rate of pay the employee would have received had he or she still been employed. In addition, the employee is credited with vesting for the time missed. However, forfeitures would not be added to the employee's account for the period.

VESTING

24. What are the vesting rules for ESOPs?

In all defined contribution and defined benefit plans, vesting must be complete when the employee reaches normal retirement age, defined as the retirement age specified in the plan or the later of the time the participant reaches age 65 and has five years of participation in the plan.

Employees must also be fully vested in the case of a full or partial plan termination.

Plans are not required to do so, but many provide for full vesting upon disability, death or reaching the early retirement age specified under the plan.

Vesting requirements depend on four factors:
1. Whether the contributions are made for plan years that start after December 31, 2006, or,

2. If there are shares acquired by an ESOP loan in effect as of September 26, 2005, or,
3. Whether the plan is top-heavy or,
4. Whether the plan is being used under the safe-harbor test for matching contributions to 401k plan.

For contributions made in plan years starting before 2006 or meeting the outstanding loan test (points 1 and 2 above), employees must "vest" (earn a non-forfeitable right to their account balances) according to one of two schedules or faster. One schedule ("cliff vesting") allows no vesting for the first five years of service, then 100% vesting at the end of the fifth year. A second schedule allows graduated vesting to begin at 20% after the third year and increase 20% per year thereafter. Faster vesting is allowed. Faster vesting is required for top-heavy plans.

However, for contributions made before December 2006, any matching contributions (including those made as part of an ESOP/401k contribution) must vest on a schedule faster than normal ESOP vesting rules. They either must fully vest after three years of service (cliff vesting) or start at not less than 20% per year after the second year of service and continue until 100% vesting is reached after six years. If the ESOP is being used to make a match to a 401k plan to meet the safe harbor test, the rules are stricter, as described separately below.

For contributions made in plan years starting after December 31, 2006, all defined contribution plans must vest their shares no later than after three years for cliff vesting and six years for graded vesting, starting at no less than 20% per year after two years of service. If there is an ESOP loan in place as of September 26, 2005, the new rules do not apply to shares acquired by the loan for any plan year beginning on the earlier of the date the loan is fully repaid or the date on which the loan was scheduled to be repaid as of September 26, 2005. There is no consensus yet on whether this exception applies only to the shares acquired by the loan or any shares in the plan as of this date. Our recommendation is to take the more cautious approach and limit the exception to the shares acquired by the loan, but the literal language of the law can be read differently.

Faster vesting schedules are required if plans are top heavy. Faster vesting is also required if the company is using the safe harbor matching contribution rule that allows companies to avoid anti-discrimination testing by making minimum contributions to the 401k plan, in which case contributions must vest immediately. These safe harbor rules allow a company to avoid testing if it contributes at least 3% of pay to all participants (regardless of what they defer) or a 100% match for the first 3% employees defer and a 50% match for deferrals between 3% and 5% of pay. In that case, these contributions must vest immediately.

If the ESOP is used as a 401k match in a plan with an automatic enrollment feature, still other rules apply. The new automatic enrollment provisions for 401k plans in the Pension Protection Act provide that companies can meet the 401k testing rules if they provide automatic enrollment (that is, employees opt out instead of opting in) that has the following features:

1. There are matching or non-elective employer contributions to the plan of not less than at least 3% of pay for all participants, regardless of deferrals or a match, or at least a 100% match for the first year and 50% match for the next 5% deferred. The matching percentage test applies to deferrals of non-highly compensated employees.

2. Employees agree to a minimum salary deferral of 3% in the first year, 4% in the second, and 5% in the third. If these rules are met, the vesting for the employer contributions can be two years, rather than immediate, as in the existing safe harbor match for contributions to 401k plans without automatic enrollment.

There is wide consensus in the retirement planning community that employees are not deferring enough into 401k plans, and too many eligible participants do not participate at all. Automatic enrollment generally results in a significant increase in participation and deferrals. The new safe harbor test is effective for plan years after December 31, 2007.

25. Do prior years of service before an ESOP is set up count towards vesting?

Prior years of service do not have to count, unless the ESOP replaces a previous plan within five years, in which case prior service must be counted. However, companies can and usually do count (or give partial credit for) years of service prior to the establishment of the ESOP and years of service prior to an individual's participation in the ESOP.

26. Can the vesting schedule be changed?

Vesting schedules can be changed in a non-discriminatory fashion, but note that participants with at least three years of service have the right to have their benefits calculated under a plan's existing vesting schedule if the plan is changed to amend the vesting schedule.

9

LEVERAGED ESOPS

*M*ost ESOPs used in Succession Planning are Leveraged ESOPs, meaning that the ESOP borrows money. There are two common sources of ESOP loans: (1) "senior debt" borrowed from a bank and (2) "subordinated debt" typically in the form of a promissory note issued to the selling shareholder(s).

Here is the process:

- The bank loan generally is made to the company.
- The company re-lends the money to the ESOP.
- The ESOP uses the loan proceeds to purchase stock from selling shareholders(s).

The promissory note issued to the selling shareholder(s) is referred to as "subordinated debt." In the case of loan default, the senior lender has priority over the subordinated lender. Suppose we have a total debt of $10 million ($5 million of senior debt and $5 million of subordinated debt). The Company has severe financial difficulties and defaults on the loan at a time when the Company has only $6 million of assets. The senior lender would receive the $5 million it is owed, while the seller would receive only $1 million of the $5 million he is owed.

There are other sources of debt financing, such as mezzanine lenders, and there is the potential, in certain limited situations, to fund an ESOP with equity. The most common source of equity financing is a strategy referred to as "lateral transfer," in which the company allows 401k participants to use a portion of their 401k plan assets to purchase stock in the ESOP.

Assume a $10 million stock purchase price. If 401k participants elect to transfer $4 million of their $12 million of plan assets to their ESOP accounts to purchase stock (lateral transfer), the ESOP would need to borrow and repay only $6 million. Due to securities law considerations, lateral transfer ESOPs are ever more complex and, therefore, even more expensive than traditional leveraged ESOPs.

The Q&As that follow discuss many aspects of leveraged ESOPs.

OVERVIEW

1. Who can lend to an ESOP?

Anyone can lend to an ESOP, as long as the transaction is at least as favorable to the plan as an arm's-length transaction. While commercial banks are the most common sources of finance, sellers of stock, the company itself, insurance companies, brokerage firms and investment bankers all can and do loan to ESOPs.

COMPANY DEBT SERVICE LIMITATIONS

2. Is there a limit on the term of repayment of an ESOP loan?

There is generally no limit on its term; however, the law requires that companies release and allocate shares based on one of two methods: the amount of principal paid each year or the amount of principal and interest. The principal only method requires that the release and allocation follow a formula that would not be slower than what a normal amortization would produce over 10 years. As a result, loans over 10 years typically use the principal plus interest method.

The real limit on ESOP loan terms is practical. Few lenders will go beyond five to seven years, although companies do occasionally obtain longer terms or longer amortization schedules.

In addition, ERISA and the Code require that any ESOP loan be primarily for the benefit of plan participants. Any loan amortization schedule longer than a normal schedule would have to be justified as being in the interest of plan participants, not primarily the company or its other owners. For instance, extending an ESOP loan from seven years to 15 years so that the payments would fit within Section 415 limits would clearly be acceptable. Extending it so that the company could keep its annual debt burden down probably would not be, in itself, an acceptable reason.

3. **Who, typically, is the borrower in an ESOP transaction and what are the rules governing the Outside and Inside Loans?**
Generally, ESOP loans involve a lender loaning money to a company, and the company loaning that to the ESOP. The terms of the two loans do not have to be the same, provided that the internal loan meets the fiduciary standards for ESOPs.

Two issues would be paramount here. First, the loan rate would have to be an arm's-length equivalent, generally meaning it would have to be no higher than the external loan rate. Second, while the term can be longer, the fiduciaries must be able to show that extending the loan is for the benefit of plan participants.

The most typical application of this would be when loan repayments on the terms of the external loan would exceed the maximum allowable amounts that can be added to employee accounts each year. By extending the term of the inside loan, the company is able to fund the ESOP; otherwise, it would either have no plan at all, or the ESOP would have to acquire fewer shares. Either of these would arguably not be in the interests of employees.

In other cases, the loan limits are not a problem, but the company wants to spread the ESOP benefit over a longer period of time. For instance, the company may be repaying the outside loan over five years, which would translate into 25% of eligible pay each year (or more if dividends and distributions are used).

Deciding just how long to extend is a facts-and-circumstances issue, but should always be approved by the plan fiduciary as in the best interests of plan participants. For very long internal loans (over 10 years, for instance), we recommend that companies not normally delay distributions until after the loan is repaid, as the loan allows, but instead follow the normal distribution schedule. To do otherwise makes it appear the company is using the extended internal loan term mostly to manage its cash for its own benefit.

SELLER FINANCING

4. Can a seller finance an ESOP loan?
Sellers can finance ESOP loans, provided the transaction is at a rate and on terms no less favorable to the ESOP than an arm's-length equivalent transaction. We refer to such arrangements as Seller Financed ESOPs and we refer to the promissory note issued by the ESOP to the Seller as a Seller Note.

5. If the seller makes an ESOP loan, does the seller still qualify for "Section 1042" rollover treatment?
Yes, but only to the extent the seller reinvests within the 15-month period (from three months before the sale to 12 months after). What this means is that, for instance, if the seller sells to the ESOP for $2 million, financing the sale with a five-year note, the seller can reinvest up to $2 million during the 15-month period in Qualified Replacement Property (see Chapter 11 Q&As 10-19) and defer taxation. The IRS does not care if the $2 million is actually the $2 million from the sale.

The problem for most sellers is that they do not have the $2 million from the sale yet, so this only works if other funds are available. The seller can, of course, just reinvest what funds are available and pay capital gains on the rest. In some cases, the seller may be able to use the note as an asset against which to borrow funds from a broker to buy replacement securities, although this will likely apply in only special circumstances.

The most popular solution to this problem is for the seller to borrow money from a bank to buy a long-term floating rate note bond, using that as the qualified replacement property.

Only the principal payments on the loan to the ESOP can be used for reinvestment purposes; the interest must be treated as such and taxes must be paid on it.

COMPANY FINANCING

6. **Can the company finance all or part of the ESOP using its own cash?**

A company can lend the money to an ESOP itself, assuming it has the cash. The transaction must be an arm's-length equivalent, meaning it is not less favorable to the ESOP than a conventional loan would be.

Company-financing makes sense if the company does not have an alternative use for the money that would generate a better after-tax return than the company would pay for an ESOP loan. For instance, if the company could borrow at 8%, and is in a 34% tax bracket, its after-tax cost of borrowing is 5.28% (8% minus the tax rate times the borrowing rate, or 8% x 34%). If the company can use the cash on hand to generate a better after-tax return than that, it makes sense to borrow the money from a lender.

7. **Can an ESOP be financed by a line of credit?**

ESOP loans must have a definite term, so the loan to the ESOP itself cannot be a line of credit. However, most ESOPs are financed by an outside loan to the company, which loans the money to the ESOP, but not necessarily on the same terms. So the outside loan could be a line of credit. The specific structuring of these loans can become complicated, so seeking professional advice is essential.

ALTERNATIVE SOURCES OF FINANCING

8. **Aside from loans, what other sources of funds can finance an ESOP?**

There are a variety of other sources of capital, including employee wage concessions and investments by managers or outsiders. Employee investments are another potential source (although this will require a securities registration in some cases and disclosure in all cases).

Bond financing is available as well. This would be used in large transactions and would involve selling bonds to the public, usually through an investment banker.

In some cases, funds from existing benefit plans can be transferred as well. See Q&As 10-13.

9. **Can employee benefit funds be used for an ESOP purchase?**

They can, but great care must be exercised. Excess funds from a defined benefit plan can be used, for instance. If a defined benefit plan has more assets than it needs to pay its obligations, the plan can be terminated and the excess go back to the employer. There is a 50% excise tax on the reversion if the company keeps it (plus income tax), but only a 20% excise tax if it goes into an ESOP.

Funds in a profit sharing plan or the employer contributions to a 401k plan can be used. Because of fiduciary issues, however, it is not advisable to put all the assets into the ESOP. If the company does poorly, participants could sue the fiduciaries for making a bad investment choice. Most advisors recommend not putting more than 30% of the plan assets into an ESOP. Alternatively, employees can be given the fiduciary decision for their own accounts. This could raise securities issues, however. This part of the law is ambiguous. If employees are given the choice, the fiduciary issue eases, but careful design of the offering to employees is a must.

10. Can funds from a defined benefit plan be used to fund an ESOP?

Using defined benefit plan assets to fund an ESOP is possible but complex and limited. Defined benefit plans (what most people think of as pension plans) promise a specific annual benefit at retirement. Companies fund these plans for employees based on actuarial assumptions about their work force and financial assumptions about how well the pension fund assets will perform.

The only way to move assets from a defined benefit plan into a defined contribution plan (such as an ESOP) is to terminate the defined benefit plan. At that point, all participants must be fully vested, and they must receive their benefits. Normally, this is done by the employer purchasing annuity contracts (a form of insurance providing employees with whatever their accrued benefit would equal in the form of payments to start at normal retirement age). If annuity contracts are not purchased, the benefit must be paid out as specified by the plan.

If, after all these benefits are fully paid, there is additional money in the fund, this excess can revert to the employer or to a replacement plan. If the employer keeps the money, it is taxable as income, plus there is a 50% excise tax. If it is rolled into a qualified replacement plan, of which the ESOP is one, it is still taxable as income, but the excise tax is only 20%. Amounts of 25% or more of the converted assets that go into the ESOP, however, would not be subject to this 20% tax or the 50% tax. Amounts in the ESOP would be allocated according to the formula. If there is more than can be allocated in any year due to annual contribution limits, the excess goes into a reversion suspense account and continues to be allocated until no funds are left.

A defined benefit plan's excess assets cannot be reverted in the first five years of the pension plan's operations.

In theory, it is also possible to convert a defined benefit plan into an ESOP. The defined benefit plan would be terminated and all participants would have to be able to choose whether to receive the full value of their distributions or have them rolled into the ESOP. Because this is a securities election, it is subject to all securities laws.

Because of all these restrictions, reversions from defined benefit plans into ESOPs are unusual.

11. Can funds in a 401k plan be used to help fund an ESOP?

Most 401k plans have two parts: the part made up of employer matches and the part made up of employee contributions. The considerations for the employer match part would be exactly the same as the considerations for moving profit sharing assets. (See Q&A 13.) For the employee part, we believe the fiduciary should not move the employee money on its own accord, although there is no explicit statutory requirement on this. The fiduciary risks for moving employee contributed money are substantial, and the IRS has not issued letters of determination specifically approving these plans. Employees could be given a choice about moving their assets, but this would almost certainly involve securities issues.

12. Can money from IRAs (Individual Retirement Account) help fund an employee ownership plan?

Funds in an IRA can be invested in anything the holder of the account wants. An IRA participant could use his or her account funds to buy company stock. This purchase would be subject to securities rules, however. To avoid expensive legal requirements, this option should be limited to accredited (generally, highly paid) individuals. The funds for these people to buy company stock could come from a terminated profit sharing or 401k plan, provided these funds can be rolled over into an IRA and then reinvested in company stock. That would allow these individuals to buy company stock on a pre-tax basis.

13. Can we use funds in an existing profit sharing plan to fund part of an ESOP acquisition?

It is possible to use funds from a profit sharing plan to fund a purchase of shares by an ESOP, but this application does raise potential problems. One way to move the funds would be for the plan's fiduciary unilaterally to decide to do so. The problem here is that the funds in the profit sharing plan are invested in a diversified portfolio, while in the ESOP they will be in a single investment. If that investment does poorly, or even fails to do as well as a prudently created portfolio would, the fiduciary can be sued for misusing employee assets.

To avoid this problem, some companies give employees a choice about whether to move their profit sharing funds into the ESOP, usually allowing them to move part or all of them. There are potential problems. First, the amount of funds employees move may not be sufficient to purchase the shares. Second, employees are making an investment decision in doing this, and securities law is unclear on whether this requires a registration if the various exemptions for securities laws are not met.

In one case (Heinold Hog), the Securities and Exchange Commission allowed a one-time election without registration, and many advisors believe this would be the case for other transactions. Even if registration is not required, however, full and objective disclosure certainly is. That can be an expensive process, often running well into five figures. It also requires the disclosure of executive salaries and other data the company may not want to make available. Finally, there is an issue about whether it is advisable, even by means of holding an election, to encourage employees to move diversified assets into company stock, especially if those diversified assets represent a significant part of their retirement.

Most ESOP advisors, therefore, recommend that at most 15% to 30% of profit sharing assets be moved to an ESOP, and that the decision be made by the fiduciary with appropriate advice from independent financial experts. Even then, the funds should only be moved if there is good reason to believe the company's stock will be a good long-term investment relative to other investments. The decision should not be made just because the ESOP needs the funds.

As noted in question 12, an alternative strategy would be to terminate a 401k or profit sharing plan, let employees roll their assets into an IRA, then have higher-paid employees buy company stock individually. This would not, however, get stock into the ESOP.

14. In a large ESOP buyout, what would a typical finance structure be?

A line of credit would be used to finance inventory and accounts receivable and would represent about 15-35% of the total. Typically, these loans have 1-3-year terms and are at the prime rate up to prime plus 2%. Short-term debt might account for 25-50% of the total, have a term of 5-10 years, and a rate of prime to prime plus 2%. Both line of credit and short-term debt usually come from a bank.

Subordinated debt would account for 10-25% of the total, would have a longer term than the other debt (7-12 years) and would be second-in-line if the company defaulted. Because of its greater risk, it gets a higher return, generally 3-7% above prime, often with an equity kicker (a way to translate debt into stock) worth 15-25% of the stock. Special mezzanine finance companies have been formed for this kind of ESOP debt, which also comes from insurance companies, finance companies, sellers or the state. This part of the transaction may also be financed by the seller taking preferred stock, which is much like subordinated debt. It carries a high fixed dividend plus an equity value that varies less than the common stock. Finally, equity investors put in cash, seeking a 30-40% annual return and look for 10-20% of the total stock.

These numbers can vary considerably by transaction, and each player may not be involved. The transaction can be greatly simplified if the company is very healthy, has little debt and good assets and/or the seller(s) is very cooperative. Under these circumstances, it is even possible to finance 100% of a transaction with a leveraged ESOP, although this is unusual.

15. How is equity allocated in a multi-investor leveraged buyout?

This varies considerably. Cash investors naturally want more for their dollar than the ESOP, which borrows money to be repaid out of future corporate earnings with much less risk to the participants (they can only lose what they might get in the future). Higher risk investors (subordinated lenders, for instance) will also want a bigger return for their dollar if they have an equity kicker as part of their investment. On the other hand, if employees take concessions, this makes them more like cash investors.

The Labor Department's view is that every dollar counts the same. If the ESOP puts up $10 million through borrowing and a cash investor

$10 million, each should get 50% of the stock. The reality is that such an approach will not attract equity investors. This regulatory situation has caused a decline in multi-investor ESOP transactions. Those that do get structured usually work through giving equity investors a different class of stock, warrants or options. Another approach gaining popularity is to have the ESOP purchase preferred stock, which would carry a higher initial value than the common, thus allowing the ESOP to pay more for it than other investors pay for common. This is a very complicated area and should be approached with only the most sophisticated of advisors.

LOAN COLLATERAL

16. What sort of collateral do lenders require?
Lenders look for much the same collateral they would seek in a conventional loan, but if a seller is selling to an ESOP and there is insufficient collateral, they may also ask for the seller's replacement security investments (the stocks and bonds the seller buys with the proceeds of the sale) to be pledged against the loan.

17. What serves as collateral for an ESOP loan?
The stock the ESOP acquires with the loan proceeds generally serves as the collateral. In practice, an ESOP loan is usually structured so that the lender loans to the company, which reloans to the ESOP. The lender then secures collateral from the company or, in some cases, from the seller. If the loan is made directly to the ESOP, the company would normally guarantee the loan, or the seller would pledge collateral for the loan.

18. Can an employer take a deduction for contributions to a loan committed to in one year but actually paid in the next?
Yes, provided the loan is committed in the prior year, contributions are committed (but not actually paid) in the prior year, and compensation

for the prior year is used as the basis for making the allocations.

19. Are there circumstances under which a company cannot deduct the full 25% of the payroll of company employees or ESOP participants to pay the principal on the ESOP loan?

Yes. First, the payroll can only include people actually in the plan. For instance, if a seller sells to an ESOP and does not participate in the plan because of the rollover rules, the seller's pay cannot be included.

Second, not more than one-third of the allocations can go to highly compensated employees, as defined by the Internal Revenue Code. If this happens, allocation rules need to be changed. If that means there is an excess because all the allocations cannot be made without violating the maximum individual allocation limits (25% of pay or $49,000 in 2009 dollars, whichever is less), the remainder can generally be placed in a suspense account to be allocated later.

Third, payroll does not include amounts over $245,000 per year in 2009 dollars, indexed by inflation, for an individual employee.

Finally, for plan years starting after December 31, 2001, eligible pay is defined to include employee deferrals into 401k plans or cafeteria plans. This limit applies to the total amount of a company's contributions to its defined contribution plans (ESOPs, stock bonus plans, profit sharing plans and 401k plans); contributions to defined benefit plans do not count towards this limit. However, in a 2004 private letter ruling, the IRS concluded that this 25% of pay limit is, for an ESOP in a C corporation, in addition to contributions by the company to other qualified plans. The maximum annual addition to any one individual's account under the plans cannot exceed the lesser of 100% of pay or $49,000 in 2009, to be indexed for inflation in $1,000 increments thereafter.

In C corporation ESOPs, dividends used to repay a loan do not count towards either the maximum deductible employer contribution or the maximum amount that can be added to an employee's account. Employee deferrals do count towards the 100% of pay or maximum dollar limitation. Annual additions thus include all employer and employee contributions to defined contribution plans. In S corporations, interest payments and forfeitures count towards the maximum annual addition limits, and interest payments count towards the 25% of pay maximum deductible employer contribution. For more detail on S corporations, see Chapter 11: S Corporation ESOPs.

20. Is there a way to contribute more than 25% of pay in a leveraged ESOP to repay a loan?

In C corporations, reasonable dividends paid on ESOP shares acquired with the loan proceeds generally can be used to repay the loan and are not included in the 25% calculation. In addition, in a 2004 private letter ruling, the IRS concluded that this 25% of pay limit is, for an ESOP in a C corporation, in addition to contributions by the company to other qualified plans. If a company maintains another defined contribution plan, the contribution limits for each plan count separately. For instance, a company could contribute up to 50% of pay. This only applies to leveraged C corporation ESOPs, however.

21. What counts as eligible pay or eligible compensation to receive an ESOP allocation?

When calculating eligible pay, the limit is $245,000 in 2009, indexed for inflation after that in $5,000 increments. Employee deferrals into cafeteria or 401k plans count as eligible pay.

In 2007, the IRS made some additional changes. The rules now provide that pre-tax elective deferrals under Code Sections 401k, 403(b), 457, 125, and 132(f)(4), as well as certain amounts for totally disabled participants under Section 22(e)(3) qualify as compensation.

Generally, payments made after severance are excluded from compensation, but payments made within 2½ months after severance for accumulated sick leave, vacation or other paid time count, as well as payments that would have been paid absent severance for work outside normal working hours, commissions, bonuses, etc.

22. What funds can be used to repay an ESOP loan?

An ESOP loan can be repaid with contributions from the company, dividends on the ESOP shares acquired by the loan (except for certain pre-1989 loans where dividends on shares in the ESOP not acquired by the loan in question can be used as well) and earnings from other investments of the trust contributed in prior years.

23. Can a company prepay an ESOP loan in excess of the Section 415 limits?

A company cannot make contributions in excess of the Section 415 limits, other than through dividends. Loan prepayments could be made from the company to the lender, but the internal loan from the company to the ESOP could not mirror this prepayment.

SHARE ALLOCATION

24. When a company makes a contribution to an ESOP trust to repay an ESOP loan, what happens to the shares in the trust? How are shares in a leveraged ESOP allocated?

Each year, as the loan is repaid, a percentage of shares held in the ESOP trust equal to the percentage of the loan that has been repaid that year is released from what is called the ESOP suspense account. The shares are then allocated to employee participant accounts. The dividends or distributions paid on allocated shares must release a number of unallocated shares with a value at least equal to the dividend or distribution.

Distributions or dividends on unallocated shares would release the number of shares paid for. For distributions or dividends paid on allocated shares, the company must allocate the released unallocated shares based on relative share balances of participants; for dividends or distributions paid on unallocated shares, the shares can be allocated on relative share balance or the company's normal allocation formula.

25. How is stock allocated in an ESOP?

Most companies allocate stock based on compensation (typically defined as the amount on the employee's W-2 tax form), plus elective deferrals under Section 401k plans and cafeteria plans. That is, each participant in the plan gets a percentage of the total shares allocated equal to that participant's percentage of total eligible pay. Eligible pay excludes pay in excess of $245,000 per year in 2009 (to be indexed for inflation in $5,000 increments after that). While W-2 compensation is the norm, compensation could also be defined to exclude bonuses or other add-ons to pay, provided the effect is not to push allocations more towards more highly paid people. About two-thirds of all ESOPs allocate on relative pay.

26. How do companies calculate the number of shares to be released each year in a leveraged ESOP?

The company can use one of two formulas, the principal only method or the principal and interest method.

The principal only method releases the percentage of the shares that is equal to the percentage of the total principal paid. This method cannot be used unless the payments of principal and interest on the loan are no less rapid than level annual payments of principal and interest over a 10-year loan, using standard amortization tables to determine allowable interest rates.

The principal and interest method releases shares based on a formula.

The number of shares held in the suspense account just before the release is multiplied by a fraction, the numerator of which is the principal and interest payments for the year and the denominator of which is the principal and interest payments remaining on the loan, including the current year. In other words, shares are allocated based on the total amount of the remaining loan (principal and interest) paid that year. The number of years on the loan must be fixed, not variable, renewal or extensions of the loan cannot be considered and the interest rate is the rate that applies at the end of the year involved.

The principal only method releases shares more slowly, in most cases, and is often preferred by banks.

27. Does the value of the contribution used to repay principal on an ESOP loan or the value of the shares released from the suspense account count as the amount allocated to an employee's account for that year?

The amount of the principal repaid is used to calculate the value of the employer contribution for the annual addition calculation. The IRS also allows companies to use the value of the shares released. Normally if the share value is lower.

28. Does the value of the contribution used to repay principal on an ESOP loan or the value of the shares released from the suspense account count as the employer's tax-deductible contribution to the ESOP?

The amount of the principal repaid is used to calculate the value of the employer contribution.

ALLOCATING DIVIDENDS

29. How are ESOP dividends allocated?

The ESOP of a closely held company typically has one annual allocation date, which is the last day of the plan year. However, the dividend record date is usually some other date within the plan year. If the dividend is to be paid to all ESOP participants, an interim allocation or calculation will need to be done in order to determine the total shares held by the ESOP on the record date, the shares allocated to each participant on the record date and the shares unallocated as of the record date.

Distributions and terminations that have occurred after the preceding allocation date will affect the allocation of dividends. If a participant terminates after the dividend record date, that person will be entitled to his or her share of the dividend even if the individual has received a distribution before the date the dividend is actually paid. However, if a participant has received a distribution of his or her entire vested account balance before the dividend record date, he or she will not be entitled to any portion of the dividend. If a participant is due a distribution under the plan, it may be helpful if the distribution is made before the declaration date or after the record date so that it is clear as to how to treat that participant for dividend purposes.

If a terminated participant has received a cash distribution from the ESOP in lieu of vested shares, the dividends attributable to those shares will be allocated to the participants who receive the shares pursuant to an exchange transaction on the next allocation date of the plan. Dividends attributable to the terminated participant's forfeitable shares (if any) will become a part of the forfeiture. The plan document and/or loan documents should address the use of dividends and how to allocate them under various circumstances.

30. How are ESOP dividends used to make exempt loan payments?

It is important to be able to identify whether the cash dividend is used to make principal payments or interest payments on an ESOP loan. The dividend should be clearly designated as to its use (either principal, interest or both). In most cases, the corporation desires the entire dividend to be applied to principal payments, thus allowing a greater contribution to be made. The IRS has informally stated that it may require ESOP sponsors to prorate the dividends between principal and interest when dividends are used for debt payments. An ESOP sponsor should consult with an ESOP attorney before assuming that the dividend can be used wholly to pay principal.

31. How are shares released by dividends allocated?

The ESOP administrator must determine the number of shares released by each source of debt payment (contributions, dividends paid on allocated shares, dividends paid on unallocated shares, etc.).

Dividends on Allocated Shares

The number of shares released attributable to the dividend payment on allocated shares (rather than the cash dividend itself) is then allocated to participants' accounts that hold the corresponding shares. If the cash dividend attributable to allocated shares is used to repay an exempt loan, the account of any participant entitled to the dividend must receive an allocation of employer securities with a fair market value not less than the amount of the entitled dividend. This allocation must be made in the year the cash dividend would otherwise have been allocated.

If the fair market value of the shares released by dividends paid on allocated shares is less than the value of the dividends themselves, additional shares must be allocated to the participants' accounts to make up the difference. To date, very little guidance has been issued by the IRS that would tell the administrator how to make up for the shortfall. A current practice is to use the shares released from the dividends paid on unallocated stock to make the participants' whole. Any remaining shares released by dividends on unallocated stock can be allocated according to a formula provided by the plan document.

The above method for making up the shortfall is frequently used because the company cannot make an additional contribution without exceeding the Code Section 415 limits. If, however, an additional contribution is made to correct a shortfall, the allocation of the shares so released must pass the general test under the nondiscrimination rules of Code Section 401(a)(4).

Dividends on Unallocated Shares
Shares released attributable to dividend payments on unallocated stock are allocated according to instructions in the plan document. Some examples of formulas that the plan may specify are: (1) allocate such shares in the same fashion as the contribution (usually according to eligible compensation), (2) allocate such shares according to the allocated shares held at the dividend record date or (3) allocate such shares according to the total account balance at the dividend record date (including any other investments account). Whatever the approach, the plan may not discriminate in favor of the highly compensated employees.

If dividends on unallocated shares are used to make up a shortfall in shares on allocated shares, any shares remaining after the corrective allocation may be allocated according to the formula provided by the plan document.

32. Can dividends be paid on both allocated and unallocated shares to repay an ESOP loan?

Yes, dividends can be paid on both allocated and unallocated shares to repay an ESOP loan. Dividends paid in this way would release additional shares for allocation to employee accounts. In effect, they are repaying the loan faster, so more shares would be released from the suspense account in an amount equal to the dividends paid. Dividends paid on unallocated shares would trigger an allocation from the suspense account based on the company's normal allocation formula; dividends paid on allocated shares would release shares from the suspense account based on the size of the dividend attributable to a participant's allocated amount.

33. What is a reasonable dividend?

The term "reasonable dividend," has never been precisely defined by regulation or statute, but most consultants believe it should be consistent with what similarly profitable companies would pay on their shares and must not create excessively high compensation for employees. Also, the company must be capable of making the dividend payment on a recurring basis.

34. When may the dividend deduction be taken?

The deduction is allowed for the corporation's taxable year during which the dividend is used, as described below:

If the dividend is paid directly to plan participants or their beneficiaries, the deduction is allowed for the taxable year in which the dividend is actually paid.

If the dividend is passed through the ESOP, the ESOP must pay plan participants or beneficiaries no later than 90 days after the close of the plan year in which it received the dividends. The deduction is allowed for the corporate tax year in which the ESOP pays recipients.

If the dividend is used to make payments on an exempt loan, the deduction is allowed for the corporate tax year in which the loan payment using those dividends is made.

10

SECTION 1042 TAX-FAVORED SALES PROCEEDS

*I*n 1984, Congress enacted legislation that allows owners of closely held C corporation stock to sell their stock to an ESOP without having to pay tax on the gain. This section of the Internal Revenue Code (1042) imposes numerous requirements that have to be satisfied in order to qualify for this tax benefit.

Section 1042, like Section 1031 dealing with real estate and Section 1035 dealing with life insurance and annuity contracts, is a like-kind exchange provision for ESOPs. The concept behind Section 1042 is that when an owner of C corporation stock sells to an ESOP for cash and then reinvests in like-kind property (other stocks and bonds), the seller will not be taxed.

However, as with other like-kind exchanges, the seller's tax basis in the securities he purchases with his ESOP proceeds is a transferred basis. For example, if you have a $100,000 tax basis in your closely held C corporation stock which you sell to an ESOP for $10 million, you will have a $100,000 basis in your $10 million reinvestment portfolio. If you subsequently sell that reinvestment portfolio for $10 million, you will trigger the $9.9 million taxable gain. Therefore, many sellers who elect 1042 treatment create their reinvestment portfolio attempting to purchase income-producing securities that they can hold until death. At death, their tax basis will be "stepped-up" and their estate will be able to sell the reinvestment portfolio without any income tax consequences.

In 1984, most incorporated businesses were structured as C corporations. Today, however, most closely held companies are structured as S corporations. Therefore, the Q&As below also discuss the potential of converting from S to a C so that the selling shareholder(s) can take advantage of 1042 tax treatment.

OVERVIEW

1. **What is a Section 1042?**

   It is a section of the Internal Revenue Code allowing sellers to certain ESOPs to defer taxation on the gain of the sale of their stock by reinvesting in other securities called qualified replacement securities.

2. **Who qualifies for Section 1042?**

   Owners of stock in closely held C corporations who have held that stock for at least three years prior to the sale. The ESOP must own 30% of the total value of shares in the company after the sale. Corporations that sell stock to an ESOP do not qualify for Section 1042, but partnerships, estates, taxable trusts and individual owners do. The shares sold to the ESOP do not qualify if they were acquired as part of an employee benefit plan or through certain types of stock options.

3. **When is tax due on the sale?**

   When the qualified replacement securities are disposed of. If only some are disposed of, then the tax is pro rata to what is sold.

4. **What happens when qualified replacement property goes into an estate?**

   To the extent the qualified replacement property has not been disposed of, there is a "step-up" in basis, so heirs pay no capital gains tax (but estate taxes are due).

5. **How long must a company stay private after taking advantage of Section 1042?**

One year. Otherwise, an excise tax is imposed on the company.

6. **Sellers to an ESOP have to hold their stock for three years prior to the sale to qualify for the Section 1042 transaction. What if their company has switched from an S to a C corporation or from a sole proprietorship or partnership to a C corporation. Will their ownership tack?**

Normally, prior ownership of a proprietorship, partnership or S corporation stock will tack to the ownership of stock in a C corporation for holding period purposes.

7. **What if the seller to an ESOP has exchanged the stock in the company for other stock, assets or partnership interest within three years before the sale to the ESOP?**

The law says the shares must have been held for at least three years before the sale to an ESOP. But what if the ESOP company had changed corporate form, say from an S corporation to a C corporation, or a partnership to a C corporation? Or what if the company had been formed last year through an exchange of stock for a previous asset? Basically, the tacking rules of the law state that if the seller had an asset or business interest that was exchanged in a tax-free transaction for stock in the company that now is setting up the ESOP, the holding period of the asset will be added to the holding period of the stock. So a partner exchanging partnership interest for stock, for example, could count ownership of both.

8. **How does a partnership sale in a Section 1042 rollover work?**

Partnerships can take advantage of Section 1042, but it is the partnership, not individual partners, who must make the choice to take the deferral and reinvest the proceeds. Once the reinvested assets are distributed to individual partners, the tax treatment is murky.

It would appear the distribution would not trigger tax, but there is no specific guidance on this. The partnership would be well advised to seek advice from the IRS beforehand. An alternative would be to distribute ownership before the sale to the ESOP and let each partner make the choice.

9. Do shares acquired from options or other employee benefit plans qualify for rollover treatment?

Sellers who got their stock through some types of stock options, an ESOP or some other compensation benefit can sell these shares to the ESOP, but they cannot defer taxes on the gain.

QUALIFIED REPLACEMENT PROPERTY

10. What kinds of securities can the seller reinvest in?

Stocks, bonds, debentures, warrants or other debt or equity instruments issued by U.S. corporations that receive not more than 25% of their income from passive investment (that is, income from investments in things other than their own business). U.S. companies are companies controlled by U.S. firms, not simply companies with operating units in the U.S. and listed on U.S. stock exchanges (Schlumberger or Food Lion, for instance, would be foreign firms). Mutual funds, U.S. government and municipal bonds, for instance, do not qualify, but banks and insurance companies do. The company can be public or private and can be owned by the seller to the ESOP. It cannot be owned by the company sponsoring the ESOP.

11. What procedural requirements apply to the purchase of qualified replacement property?

The seller must purchase qualified replacement property within 12 months after the sale or three months prior to it. The seller must obtain a notarized statement of purchase within 30 days of the purchase of these properties. In addition, the seller must file an irrevocable statement of election on or before the tax return due date for the tax year in which the sale occurs. This election must describe the securities sold to the ESOP, the sale date, the adjusted basis of the shares, the amount for which they sold, the identity of the ESOP that purchased the shares and information about the sale of securities to parties other than the ESOP if the sale was part of a larger transaction. Finally, there must be a statement of consent by the company to the election.

These forms are not available from the government, but most brokerage firms, ESOP advisors or law firms handling the 1042 transaction will have their own version of the forms.

12. Can a seller in a 1042 transaction invest in a new company?

Yes, with certain requirements. As long as:

- the seller buys securities in the new company;
- the new company is not a member of the same control group as the company whose shares the seller sold to the ESOP, and
- it is a domestic operating company.

Advisors suggest, however, investing in safer securities and borrowing against them to invest in a new company.

13. Is there any way for the seller to buy and trade securities without paying tax?

There are a number of long-term (30- to 60- year) non-callable bonds specially designed for the ESOP rollover investment. Because they are non-callable (the issuer cannot buy them back at its discretion), the buyer can feel secure that they can be held until death without triggering a disposition (as a call would be considered), and having to pay tax.

The buyer of these bonds can borrow against them for up to 75% to 90% of their face value. The borrowed funds can then be used to buy and sell whatever the buyer wants. The buyer pays tax when these investments are sold, but only based on their increase in value.

This strategy may or may not be attractive. The long-term bonds typically pay a variable rate lower than other long-term interest rates. The loan interest rate is often somewhat higher than the bond interest rate. Although the loan rate is usually fixed, its relationship to the bond interest rate varies, and it would typically start at a point or so higher.

This means that for the strategy to work, the investor must make a return on the buy and sell strategy that is higher than the buy and hold strategy normally followed after a 1042 transaction. How much higher will vary, but it must make up for the difference between:

- the 25% of the investment that cannot be margined and that pays a relatively low interest rate, and
- the difference between the loan rate and the interest rate on the bond.

This could mean an annual rate of return of 25% to 50% higher on the borrowed funds could be needed just to break even.

14. If a seller to an ESOP buys a floating-rate note from a company that subsequently no longer qualifies as qualified replacement property (such as would happen if it started to receive too much income from passive investment), does this disqualify the investment?

No, the test is as of the date of purchase of the investment.

15. Can a seller loan to an ESOP and take advantage of Section 1042?

If a seller loans to an ESOP, he may not be able to take full advantage of the ESOP rollover provision that allows him to defer tax by reinvesting in other securities. The law specifies that a seller to an ESOP has three months before and 12 months after the sale before it has to reinvest the proceeds in securities of qualifying companies. In a seller-financed transaction, the seller may be getting paid in annual installments. The seller cannot just reinvest these installments as he or she receives them and qualify. Instead, only the amount actually reinvested during the 15-month period qualifies. As a result, the seller must have other funds to reinvest within the reinvestment period to make this work.

16. A disposition of qualified replacement securities requires the seller to pay tax. What constitutes such a disposition?

The seller pays no tax on the sale to the ESOP until the qualified replacement property is disposed of. Almost any transaction that results in the seller no longer owning the replacement securities constitutes a disposition. Usually, this means sold, but it could include other taxable exchanges, such as

- a bond that is called (bought back) by its issuer,
- a court-ordered transfer of securities pursuant to a divorce and certain exchanges of stock, or
- the disposition of partnership assets when a partnership originally made the 1042 election.

The most important exception is the transfer of the securities to a non-taxable trust, such as a charity or a family limited partnership (the partners pay tax, not the trust, in this arrangement) or a transfer to family members.

17. Are there transactions that transfer qualified replacement property that are not dispositions triggering the tax?

Yes. Disposition by gift, including to a charity, family trust or family member would not trigger the tax. Also dispositions triggered by death, the resale of the replacement property to an ESOP pursuant to Section 1042 (a very unusual circumstance that would involve reinvesting in a private firm and selling the stock to that company's ESOP) or non-taxable corporate reorganizations, such as stock-for-stock mergers or internal recapitalizations replacing one security with another of equivalent value would not trigger the tax.

18. **What is the basis for the tax when qualified replacement property is sold?**

The basis is the price paid for the shares in the company stock sold to the ESOP.

19. **When replacement securities are sold, does the sale of any of the securities trigger tax on the entire amount rolled over from the ESOP sale?**

No. Tax is due on the pro rata amount sold. Suppose the seller to the ESOP buys 10 stocks, and sells one that was worth 10% of the original value of the sale to the ESOP at the time the security was designated a "qualified replacement property." The seller would pay tax on 10% of the gain (if any) from the replacement security, using the original basis in the stock sold to the ESOP. This percentage is based on the value of the replacement property when purchased, not when sold.

30% ESOP OWNERSHIP REQUIREMENT

20. **Can a shareholder make a 1042 election if the seller sells less than 30% of the stock to the ESOP, but commits to sell enough to go over 30% later?**

No, although the statute may technically allow this, the IRS would probably not allow it.

21. **Does the ESOP have to buy 30% from one owner for the sale to qualify?**

No. Once the ESOP owns 30% of the stock, all sales, including that bringing it to 30%, qualify the seller for the rollover. For instance, if three sellers sell 30% in the same transaction, all three can take the rollover. If one sells 30%, and another sells 10% two years later, both qualify.

22. The law says that if the ESOP ownership drops below 30% within three years after a 1042 sale because of a sale or disposition of the ESOP shares, then there is a 10% excise tax on the proceeds of that sale or disposition. Are there any exceptions to this?

Yes. If the ESOP ownership drops below 30% because the company reacquires shares from departing ESOP participants or if the company is sold in a Section 368 sale (a tax free exchange of the stock in one company for the stock of another), then the tax does not apply. Note that the tax also does not apply if the ESOP ownership drops below 30% because of dilution of the shares by the issuance of new stock. It would apply, however, if someone bought shares back from the ESOP directly.

23. How do options or warrants count in meeting the 30% test for Section 1042?

The ESOP must own at least 30% of the common equity of the employer on a fully diluted basis. For instance, if there are 1,000 shares, plus options for another 200, the ESOP must end up with 360 shares (30% of 1,200), not 300 shares. However, the 30% test cannot be met by giving the ESOP options. If there are 1,000 shares outstanding, and the ESOP gets 200, plus an option on 100 more, that will not meet the 30% test. The ESOP must actually own 30% after the sale, and not merely have the right to own that percentage if it chooses to exercise the options. The calculation is the same for warrants or similar securities that can be, but have not yet been, exercised.

24. The law requires that 30% of the stock be owned by the ESOP for the rollover to apply. How does this apply when there are multiple classes of stock?

The ESOP must own 30% of the value of all classes of stock or 30% of each class.

25. **The law requires that the ESOP hold at least 30% of the value of the company's shares after the 1042 election. After a debt is taken out to buy the shares, however, the value usually declines. Is the value used for the 30% rule the pre- or post-transaction value?**

The post-transaction value.

26. **Does the pay of people who cannot get an allocation of shares due to 1042 or attribution rules still count as eligible pay in calculating the total payroll of the ESOP?**

In deciding whether to sell to an ESOP, a key factor is whether the company has enough payroll of plan participants to make the sale practical given the payroll-based limitations on what can be put into the plan. A common error is to include the pay of ineligible people in this calculation. Anyone who cannot receive an allocation, whether under 1042 rules or the attribution rules, cannot have their pay included. However, to the extent there is stock in the ESOP that is not subject to tax deferral treatment, these shares can be allocated to all employees who meet the service requirements.

PROHIBITED ALLOCATION RULE

27. **Three people are selling to an ESOP. One seller owns less than 25% of the shares and will continue to do so after the sale. Will he be eligible for any of the allocation of shares?**

Not if the seller elects the tax-free rollover. If that is not elected, then the seller can get an allocation.

28. **Suppose Person A sells shares to an ESOP but does not elect 1042. Person B and Person C also sell shares, but they do elect 1042. Can Person A get an allocation from the ESOP?**

Yes, as long as Person A is not a 25% shareholder (including allocation after the transaction).

29. Are any relatives legally considered to be owners of stock by attribution for the purposes of the limitations in Section 1042 on allocations of stock subject to the tax deferral treatment?

Yes. Attribution rules under Section 318(a)(1)(A) of the Internal Revenue Code say that stock owned by an individual is considered owned by his or her spouse, children, grandchildren and parents. People who fail to meet the 25% owner or relative tests for the purpose of Section 1042 cannot have stock subject to the rollover allocated to them nor can their pay be counted as eligible payroll for purposes of annual allocation limits. In addition, ownership of a partnership, trust, estate, employee benefit plan and subchapter S corporation is attributed to the owners or beneficiaries of these entities proportionately to their interest in them.

For instance, assume Mary and John are married and own a company. Their son Bill works for the company. Seventy percent of the ownership is in Mary's name and 30% is owned by George, the CFO. George's daughter Jill works for the company. Under attribution rules, John and Bill are considered 70% owners as well, while Jill and George are considered 30% owners. John and George would be excluded from participation in the ESOP by virtue of the 1042 rules. Jill, however, would not be excluded under 1042, but would be excluded under attribution rules (she would be considered a 25% owner). Similarly, if someone owned 20% of the company directly, and was a 50% partner in a partnership owning 30% of the company, that person would be considered a 35% owner.

There is a de minimis exception to this for allocations of up to 5% of the total ESOP shares bought in Section 1042 sales that are allocated to lineal descendants of sellers who have elected 1042 treatment. However, this exception is constrained by attribution rules in a way that essentially limits its applicability to children of owners who own 25% or less before the sale and when shares from the transaction are allocated, and to grandchildren or great-grandchildren, etc. (an owner's shares are attributed to his or her children but not the grand-children or great-grandchildren, etc.).

30. If the seller has remarried, are children of the new spouse excluded from Section 1042 stock allocations?

No, unless they have been adopted by the seller.

31. Are there any exceptions to the prohibited allocation rules?

Yes. The law says that lineal descendants of the seller can, collectively, receive an allocation of up to 5% of the ESOP shares. This exception has an exception, however. Attribution rules (See question 29.) require the ownership of parents to be considered owned by the children. If the seller to the ESOP is more than a 25% owner, therefore, the seller's children cannot get stock despite the de minimis rule because they are prohibited as 25% owners. So who can benefit from this rule (other than attorneys)? Children of less than 25% owners who sell to an ESOP owning more than 30% of the company and grandchildren of any qualified seller would be the only obvious beneficiaries. Note that this is the unofficial position of the IRS; some practitioners disagree.

ALTERNATIVE TO 1042: CHARITABLE REMAINDER TRUSTS

32. Aside from the bond strategy, are there other ways to diversify a 1042 holding?

The seller could contribute the funds to a charitable remainder trust, which would take the value of the securities and give the donor an annual income. The charity keeps the securities, however, so this only works for people with a charitable intent.

11

S CORPORATION ESOPS

An S corporation is a flow through entity, meaning that the company does not pay income tax. Rather, its earnings flow through to its shareholders who pay tax on the company's earnings.

Since an ESOP's shares are owned by the ESOP's tax-exempt trust known as the Employee Stock Ownership Trust or ESOT, when the company's earnings are flowed through to the ESOT, they are not taxed. To the extent of the ESOT's ownership, that percentage of the company's income is free of federal taxation. For example, if an ESOT owns 100% of a company's stock, the company will operate, essentially, as a tax-exempt entity.

S corporations were not allowed to sponsor ESOPs until the law was changed in 1996 and then revised in 1998. Just a few years later, a group of promoters from outside the mainstream of the ESOP industry developed a scheme to take advantage of the tax benefits of a 100% ESOP owned S corporation without actually sharing the value of the company with its employees. This scheme was shut down by Congress in the 2001 tax act in a provision known as the S Corporation ESOP Anti-Abuse Rules (Section 409(p) of the Internal Revenue Code).

The Q&As that follow discuss S corporation taxation, S corporation ESOPs and the S corporation ESOP Anti-Abuse rules.

OVERVIEW

1. Can an S corporation have an ESOP?

In the past they could not, but since January 1, 1998, S corporations can have ESOPs, 401k plans, stock bonus plans and profit sharing plans own their stock. However, not all the tax benefits available to ESOPs in C corporations are available to ESOPs in S corporations.

S corporations are taxed like partnerships. That is, the gains and losses are passed directly through to the owners; the corporation does not pay tax. If an ESOP or other qualified plan were an owner, it could be a tax dodge because the plan would not be taxable.

In 1996, legislation was passed to deal with this issue. It allowed ESOPs, 401k plans, stock bonus plans and profit sharing plans to own stock in an S corporation. The employee benefit trust, however, would be responsible for its share of taxes, paid at its own tax rate. For instance, if the trust were a 20% owner, and the S corporation had $100,000 in earnings in a year, the trust would pay taxes on $20,000, taxed at the rate applicable to an individual earning $20,000 in a year (assuming the trust has no other income, which it might from non-stock investments or from the sale of assets). Presumably, the company would pay the tax by contributing the money to the plan. This contribution would not, however, need to be allocated to employee accounts. One unresolved issue is whether a distribution of stock to an employee would be deemed a gain to the trust and thus taxable to the trust (as well as to the employee).

Unfortunately, the 1996 legislation left some technical gaps that made it impractical for qualified plans actually to hold company stock in an S corporation. First, it allowed employees to take their shares at departure. If employees put these into an IRA, the S election would be voided because an IRA cannot own S corporation stock. Second, it did not provide an exemption from prohibited transaction rules under the Employee Retirement Income Security Act for sales by owner employees to a qualified plan, something that is exempted for C corporations. Finally, it was ambiguous about the tax the trust would pay on any gains in the value of the shares it held when these shares were distributed to employees. Arguably, the trust would have to pay unrelated business income tax (UBIT) on the gain, meaning the gains would be taxed twice: to the employee and the trust.

In 1997, these problems were fixed, but only for ESOPs. The owner employee exemption was added to the law, the trust was exempted from the UBIT tax and the company can require departing employees to take the cash value of their shares. Profit sharing, 401k and stock bonus plans will still face the tax problems, making their ownership of stock in an S corporation impractical.

S COMPARED TO C CORPORATION ESOPS

2. **What are the differences in tax benefits available to an S corporation ESOP and a C corporation ESOP?**
    Tax benefits available to a C corporation are:
    - deferral of taxation on the gains made from the sale to a 30% or more ESOP (the so called 1042 rollover);
    - deduction of dividends paid on ESOP shares, and
    - the ability to ignore interest payments in calculating the limit on contributions to repay an ESOP loan.

    These benefits are not available to an S corporation ESOP. Moreover, unlike a C corporation ESOP, interest payments on an ESOP loan and forfeited shares re-contributed to the ESOP would count towards the contribution limits.

    For plan years not starting after December 31, 2001, the maximum deductible limit on employer contributions to an S corporation ESOP was 15% of eligible pay. However, an ESOP could be combined with a money purchase pension plan to reach 25% of pay. A money purchase pension plan requires the company to make a non-discretionary annual contribution to the plan. That non-discretionary amount can be added to the normal 15% of eligible pay that can be contributed in a qualified plan like an ESOP or stock bonus plan. For plan years starting after December 31, 2001, the limit is 25% of pay, whether there is a money purchase plan or not. Most S corporation ESOPs that were using a money purchase plan feature have now dropped it.

3. Why would a company choose to stay Subchapter S rather than convert to a C corporation when buying out an owner?

C corporations pay tax on earnings. If any of those earnings are distributed as dividends, a second round of tax is paid by the owners. Any retained earnings are, in effect, ultimately taxed again to owners as additional capital gains as reflected in an increased share price when the stock is sold.

Subchapter S status allows a company not to pay tax at the corporate level. Instead, all earnings are allocated to owners, who pay tax on them at personal tax rates, whether they actually receive these earnings or not. Since the ESOP itself is a tax-exempt entity, to the extent the ESOP owns an S corporation, neither the corporation nor the owners pay taxes.

The advantage of S corporation ESOPs are most compelling in the following five situations:

1. The seller is not the only owner. While the seller benefits from the conversion to C status, the other owners now find any of their earnings that would have been sheltered from the corporate level tax no longer are. If the sale does not create enough deductions to reduce the corporate level tax low enough to satisfy these owners, they may not want to convert.

Note, however, that the other owners may not face this problem if the ESOP creates enough debt or contribution obligations to reduce or eliminate the corporate level tax.

2. There are large amounts of undistributed earnings. When the conversion to a C corporation takes place, any earnings that have not yet been distributed to the owners must be distributed in one year or they are taxable to the owners (meaning they will be taxed twice, since the owners have already paid tax on them before). If the company does not have the cash to do this, it could borrow money, but the ESOP may itself require too much cash to make this payout practical.

3. Remaining owners plan to sell the company in an asset sale at some time after the ESOP is implemented. In an S corporation, the sale of the company's assets triggers only a single tax at the individual level; in a C corporation, the sale would be taxed at both the corporate and individual level, as income to the company and as capital gains to the individuals. The amount of the corporate tax would depend in part on the depreciation taken on the assets.

4. The S corporation is creating losses the owners want flowed through to them. In some situations, a company may be making heavy investments, often in real property or other hard assets that create paper losses. These losses can be flowed through to the owners, who can deduct them at a marginally higher rate than can the company. In some scenarios, this may be desirable.

5. The seller's basis is already very high because of taxes paid on previously undistributed earnings. In this case, the rollover provision may not make much difference.

Having said this, however, most S corporations will find the ESOP benefits valuable enough to make a conversion to C status warranted.

4. **Does ownership in an ESOP count towards the 2% test for allowing the deductibility of fringe benefits in an S corporation?**
It does not.

5. **If an ESOP buys shares during the year in an S corporation, is the ESOP tax shield prorated to the time during which the plan was in place?**
If the ESOP owns shares for part of the year, then the tax shield applies only to that fractional part of the year in which it is an owner. Say the ESOP buys 40% of the shares in a calendar-year company on July 1. If the company's profits are $1 million, the pre-ESOP owners would pay tax on 60% of the $1 million in profits plus one half of the tax owed on the 40% they owned
for six months.

6. **In an S corporation, do forfeitures reallocated to employee accounts count toward the maximum annual addition limits?**
They do; only in C corporations can forfeitures of stock acquired by an ESOP loan not be counted.

S CORPORATION DISTRIBUTIONS/DIVIDENDS

7. **Does an ESOP in an S corporation have to receive its share of earnings distributions paid to other owners?**
Yes. S corporations typically make cash distributions of earnings to owners in amounts at least sufficient to enable these owners to pay their taxes. Even though the ESOP does not have to pay taxes on its share of earnings, it must receive a pro rata share of any distributions.

8. **When allocating distributions in an S corporation, when can an ESOP use compensation or its other normal allocation formula to make allocations?**
    Distributions on allocated shares must be based on the value of shares in each employee's account. Distributions on unallocated shares can be based either on share balances or on the company's normal allocation formula for contributions.

9. **When an S corporation makes distributions to an ESOP, what can the ESOP do with these distributions?**
    The ESOP can use these distributions to add to employee accounts, repurchase shares from departing employees or buy additional shares.

10. **Can S corporation distributions (also called dividends) be passed through to employees in an S corporation?**
    It would not be very practical. The pass through would require the consent of each employee and would be subject to taxation. It is not clear if you could allow each employee to choose to elect to get a dividend or whether they all would have to choose, but advisors say that the issues created by the pass through would not be worth the potential benefits.

11. **When S corporation distributions are used to repay an ESOP debt in an S corporation, can they be paid on both allocated and unallocated shares?**
    Yes. As a result of tax law changes passed in 2004, ESOPs in S corporations can now use distributions on allocated and unallocated shares to repay an ESOP loan. Prior to this law, an IRS private letter ruling had indicated that only distributions on unallocated shares could be used.

12. **Will distributions paid on ESOP shares in S corporations be considered as company contributions for the purposes of testing annual addition rules?**

No.

S CORPORATION ESOP ANTI-ABUSE RULES / SECTION 409(p)

13. **Can an S corporation ESOP be used primarily to benefit just one or a few employees?**

Not without serious tax penalties. In the 2001 tax act, Congress made it highly impractical to use an ESOP in an S corporation just to benefit one or a few (usually highly paid) employees. The law is somewhat complicated, but works as follows:

> 1. First, define "disqualified persons." Under the law, a disqualified person is an individual who owns 10% or more of the allocated and unallocated shares in the ESOP or who, together with family members (spouses or other family members, including lineal ancestors or descendants, siblings and their children or the spouses of any of these other family members) own 20% or more. Synthetic equity, broadly defined to include stock options, stock appreciation rights and other equity equivalents, is also counted as ownership (in effect, ESOP ownership) for this determination. Shares directly owned are not considered in determining who is a disqualified person.
>
> 2. Second, determine if disqualified individuals own at least 50% of all shares in the Company. In making this determination, ownership is defined to include:
>
>> a. shares held directly (in contrast with step 1 above);
>>
>> b. shares owned through synthetic equity, including the equivalent equity value of any deferred compensation paid out after more than 2½ years after the compensation award is granted;

    c. shares allocated to the individual's ESOP account;

    d. the individual's pro rata share of the unallocated shares owned through the ESOP.

If disqualified individuals own (or are deemed to own) at least 50% of the stock of the Company, then the Company has a "non-allocation year" and is subject to penalties. In the first non-allocation year, there is a 50% tax on the fair market value of shares allocated to all disqualified individuals even if no additional allocations are made to those individuals that year. In other words, the tax applies simply if disqualified individuals own (or are deemed to own) more than 50% of the Company in the first year.

In addition, disqualified persons may not receive allocations from the ESOP during non-allocation years without a substantial tax penalty. If such an allocation does occur, it is taxed as a distribution to the recipient and a 50% corporate excise tax would apply to the fair market value of the stock allocated. If synthetic equity is owned, a 50% excise tax would also apply to its value as well.

Finally, both an allocation to a disqualified person and the accumulation of ownership or deemed ownership of 50% or more of the stock constitutes a prohibited allocation and the plan would no longer be an ESOP.

Effective Date

For plans in existence prior to March 14, 2001, the rules became effective for plan years beginning December 31, 2004. For plans established after March 14, 2001, or for pre-existing C corporation ESOPs that switched to S status after this date, the effective date is for plan years ending after March 14, 2001.

Authorization to Disallow Existing Abuses in Plans

In addition, the Congressional conference report directed the IRS to develop regulations to define existing plans as subject to this legislation, regardless of when they were established, if their purpose is "in substance, an avoidance or evasion of the prohibited allocation rule."

14. **What happens if an employee in an S corporation ESOP accumulates more than 10% (or 20% as a family member) of the deemed owned shares? Is this accrual counted as a prohibited allocation, or must an actual allocation occur for there to be a problem?**

Existing ESOP account balances of persons owning more than the allowed amounts that are attributable to prior years constitute a prohibited allocation in a non-allocation year.

15. **Do general family attribution rules apply to the anti-abuse testing requirements in an ESOP under Section 409(p)?**

On March 12, 2005, the IRS issued a correction to regulations designed to curb abuses of ESOPs in S corporations. In those regulations, family attribution rules that generally apply in the tax law (such as considering a spouse's ownership as ownership of the other spouse) were incorporated into tests under the ESOP regulations for who is considered a disqualified person. Many ESOP experts believed that this was overly broad, and the IRS has now said it is deleting this provision.

Note that the definition of family members for the anti-abuse testing is much broader than normal definitions. Spouses, lineal ascendants and descendants, brothers and sisters-in-law, brothers and sisters and the lineal ascendants and descendants of brothers and sisters all are included. This definition applies only to who is a family member; not to whose ownership is attributed to whom.

16. What is meant by synthetic equity for purposes of S corporation anti-abuse rules?

Synthetic equity includes any rights to equity, such as phantom stock, stock options, restricted stock and stock appreciation rights, as well as claims on future resources of the company that could be characterized as equity. This includes any deferred compensation paid out more than 2½ years after its grant and equity or equity-like interests in related companies.

The counting of synthetic equity interests is a complicated matter with multiple variations depending on the scenario involved. Regulations concerning this issue take up several pages. Before issuing synthetic equity in any form, be sure to discuss the matter carefully with your advisors.

17. If an S ESOP owns less than 100% of the shares, how are synthetic deemed owned shares calculated?

The number of shares of synthetic equity as otherwise determined is reduced by multiplying that number by the percentage ownership of outstanding stock by the ESOP. This assumes the other shareholders are tax-paying persons or entities. Thus, where the ESOP owns 30% of the corporation's outstanding stock, if the number of synthetic shares owned by a person without this rule would be 100, it will only be 30 shares after application of the rule.

18. What is the measurement date for determining the value of equity compensation such as stock appreciation rights (SARs) for purposes of S corporation anti-abuse testing?

Synthetic equity in the form of stock appreciation rights is valued by determining the appreciation in value at the time of measurement.

19. **Can a company avoid the Section 409(p) anti-abuse rules by moving excess assets into another plan or buying shares in the account and transferring them to cash in the same account?**

A transfer to a profit sharing plan or other non-ESOP plan can be used. The non-ESOP plan is required to pay tax on any unrelated business taxable income attributable to the shares transferred. Shares could also be purchased and translated into cash in the ESOP account, but under temporary rules issued in 2005, that purchase would be considered an allocation and could fall under the non-allocation year rules, even though this seems like an illogical result.

20. **If options to acquire shares with additional or extra voting rights are issued, how is their value calculated for S corporation anti-abuse testing under Section 409(p)?**

Options to acquire unissued shares having more voting rights than the ESOP owned stock will be increased in proportion to the vote.

21. **If stock in an ESOP account of a disqualified person is sold, is that considered part of the allocation for the year?**

Confusingly, it appears so under temporary regulations issued in 2005.

12

ESOP VALUATIONS

*V*aluation refers to the process of determining:
1. The price the ESOP will pay for the selling shareholder(s)' stock, and
2. The price of the stock each year to be used in calculating the value of a participant's ESOP account. The value of each share multiplied by the number of shares in a participant's account equals the value of that participant's account.

The law requires that the value of shares for these purposes be determined by an "independent professional" valuation consultant. While this term has not been defined, some generally accepted guidelines have evolved.

The requirement that the valuation consultant be independent is best satisfied by having the ESOP trustee, not the company, engage the consultant. The valuation firm, ideally, should not have a prior relationship with the company or its owners. We sometimes find that business owners want the trustee to hire the company's CPA firm to perform the valuation. While the CPA firm may have the experience and expertise to qualify as a valuation professional, they likely would not be considered independent due to their relationship with the company and its owners.

The requirement that the valuation consultant be professional is best satisfied by ensuring that the consultant has the requisite credentials and that he regularly performs valuations for ESOP transactions. Generally accepted credentials include:

- Accredited Senior Appraiser (ASA), conferred by the American Society of Appraisers.
- Accredited in Business Valuation (ABV), conferred by the American Institute of Certified Public Accountants.
- Chartered Financial Analyst (CFA), conferred by the CFA Institute.
- Certified Valuation Analyst (CVA), conferred by the National Association of Certified Valuation Analysts (NACVA).

Valuation of an ownership interest in a company ultimately is a matter of informed judgment based upon a full consideration of all relevant data, as well as the appropriate standard of value. The appraisal profession recognizes three general approaches to valuation. Within each approach there are multiple methodologies. Below I have provided a very brief summary of each approach.

- The *Asset Based Approach* is based directly on the value of the assets of the business, less liabilities. This approach includes those methods that seek to write up or down or otherwise adjust the various tangible and/or intangible assets of a business.
- The *Income Approach* includes those methods that provide for the capitalization of earnings estimates and those based upon projected future benefits (cash flow or earnings) discounted to the present using an appropriate risk adjusted discount rate.
- The *Market Approach* compares the company being valued to similar companies that have been sold.

Once the valuation consultant determines the value of the company as a whole (the Enterprise Value), it then values the specific ownership interest being sold. This may result in certain valuation discounts such as the minority interest discount and the discount for lack of marketability being applied.

The Q&As that follow discuss ESOP valuations in greater detail.

OVERVIEW

1. What are the basic elements of an appraisal?

An appraiser will look at several factors. These include projected future cash flows and profits, book value, market conditions, debt, management, technology, etc. Data on comparable public companies will be collected, particularly financial ratios such as price/earnings ratios, assets/earnings ratios, etc. These ratios help determine how much the company being appraised is worth (if comparable public firms have an average 7:1 price/earnings ratio, for instance, the appraised company could be valued at a 7:1 ratio), but most appraisers also factor in net asset value and/or discounted future cash flow or earnings. The question is, "How much is the right to future revenue streams worth in terms of a lump sum today?" These factors will be blended to come up with a number to answer that question. Obviously, different appraisers will come up with different values.

From there, the appraiser will adjust the value to reflect discounts for lack of marketability if the company is private (it is harder to sell shares in a private firm than a public firm); lack of control (people pay a premium for control rights); and, for some appraisers, the repurchase obligation. How much, if any, discount is taken varies with the appraiser. For this reason, it is important to discuss these assumptions beforehand. These discounts are discussed in this section.

INDEPENDENT QUALIFIED VALUATION CONSULTANT

2. Who must perform an ESOP valuation?

An independent, outside professional. There are no standards to determine what constitutes a professional, other than, as the proposed regulations on valuation put it, someone who customarily does appraisal work. Appraisers do get certified by various appraisal organizations, but these certifications usually only involve short programs or examinations, not professional degrees or tests of detailed competence. Appraisers who are chartered financial analysts do go through a much more extensive program requiring passing very demanding exams. The term "independent" also has not been defined, but most consultants argue it should be someone with no other business relationship with the company, including the firm's CPA or an appraiser who works with a lawyer to set up the plan. Aside from these legal requirements, an appraiser should be sought based on specific ESOP experience.

3. **What sort of information will an ESOP valuation require?**
There are no legal requirements for what must be included in an ESOP valuation. For the valuation to have merit, however, most appraisers will want three to 10 years of financial statements, preferably audited or at least reviewed; three to five years of projected financial statements; interim statements as close to the valuation date as possible; a list of all lines of business, assets, off-balance sheet assets and liabilities; lists of main customers, suppliers and competitors; legal agreements affecting the company and its owners (such as by-laws and buy-sell agreements); a list of assets, capital and depreciation expenditure records; major contracts; compensation schedules; a history of any stock sales and offers, and any other information that could affect how much the company is worth.

In addition, the appraiser will want to visit the company and talk to key people. In very complex cases, interviews with customers, suppliers and industry experts could be in order, but most valuations will not take this step.

Failing to provide adequate information, or providing misleading information in a way that could affect value, is a serious offense that could lead to lawsuits by the participants or the government, as well as the loss of tax benefits and the imposition of penalties.

ESOP fiduciaries are generally responsible to make sure the valuation consultants receive the proper information.

VALUATIONS AND FAIRNESS OPINIONS

4. What is the difference between a valuation and a fairness opinion?

A valuation assesses the fair market value of the ESOP's share of the enterprise, depending on its purpose.

A fairness opinion determines the fairness of a transaction to the ESOP participants. In simple transactions, this is not an issue. Fairness is more complicated where there are multiple owners, and especially where there are different classes of stock or different groups are putting up different kinds of investments (one group cash, one group borrowing money, an ESOP borrowing money the company repays, employees putting up wage or benefit concessions, etc.).

A financial advisor is retained to advise the ESOP fiduciary to determine if the offer to buy stock is fair to all parties. The advisor will assess present and future prospects for the company, the existence of other alternatives to the sale, the ability to obtain financing for the transaction and the overall effect of the proposal on the company's various constituencies. The report may just be a letter with an opinion, outlining the methods used to arrive at the judgment.

Consider this situation: If one investor puts in $1 million in cash and the ESOP puts in $1 million with borrowed money to be repaid out of future earnings, what is a fair price for both to pay? These and similar situations call for a professional financial advisor to opine on the fairness of the transaction, but the ESOP trustee must ultimately make the decision.

Fairness opinions are not legally required in ESOP or other transactions, but are highly advisable in complex ones (See Q&A 5).

5. When specifically is a fairness opinion required?

Fairness opinions may be needed when:

1. There are competing bids that differ in terms of structure, timing or price.
2. There is an unsolicited or hostile offer for the company.
3. Directors disagree about the adequacy of an offer.
4. There is a conflict about the impact of ESOP debt on the value of the shares.
5. Shareholders express concerns that all were treated fairly.
6. Differing offers have been made to differing owners.
7. The company has done poorly in recent years, raising issues about whether it makes sense to continue to hold and/or buy employer stock.

6. What is an assessment of adequate consideration?

An assessment of adequate consideration is a statement, often by a valuation firm, that determines whether an ESOP is receiving fair market value in a proposed transaction. It is generally less involved than a full valuation and involves a determination about whether there have been sufficient changes in the company since the last valuation date to require an updated valuation.

7. Can the ESOP trustee pay more than fair market value if it decides the transaction is nonetheless worthwhile for employees?

An ESOP can never pay more than appraised market value for the shares. Sellers may be unrealistic in their assumption that they could sell the stock for more money elsewhere, however. If they want to maintain a controlling interest in the company, any other buyer will also want a hefty minority discount (if, indeed, any buyer can be found). The ESOP could pay more if the sellers are willing to give the

ESOP additional rights, such as a higher dividend on the stock (this would probably require converting ESOP shares to preferred or super common, and may not be possible in an S corporation), a right to buy control over time, tagalong rights if the sellers do sell to someone else or other rights.

TIMELINES OF VALUATION

8. For allocations, deductions, distributions and ESOP purchases, when must stock be valued in an ESOP?

The law says that ESOPs must pay no more than fair market value. By definition, a valuation that is stale is not proof that the ESOP is paying fair market value. Using a current value is usually easy to do in an ESOP purchase. The purchase is simply timed to occur very soon after the valuation.

The issue becomes trickier in distributions. Timing rules for distributions may require a distribution at a time when a valuation is several months old. The plan year may close December 31, for instance, and distributions must start 60 days after for some participants. The valuation actually might be delayed until 120 days after, usually because the company's plan and fiscal years are different. Using the previous year's valuation may be inappropriate. Ideally, a company will coordinate with the appraiser so that its valuation is completed in a timely fashion, but, if not, fiduciaries need to decide if using a previous value is appropriate. Some consultants believe companies can make distributions at the old value, but correct upwards if the subsequent valuation shows an increase. If the fiduciary has reason to believe the value has declined, however, using the old value would cause a fiduciary issue with respect to current participants. In this case, a valuation update would be required. Some consultants argue, however, that if the plan documents support this, distributions can occur at the previous year-end appraisal.

In diversification elections, most consultants believe it is acceptable to use the prior year's valuation. For deduction purposes, the valuation should be current; an update is permitted (this would involve a briefer reappraisal of the value rather than an annual appraisal).

To avoid difficulties, companies should coordinate all ESOP transactions in a way that they occur as much as possible within a close window of the valuation. If a company knows its valuation will be completed in April, for instance, its plan year could run April to April and stock contributions made in April. This may not always be practical, however.

9. **If the ESOP appraisal is not very near an ESOP transaction, what should be done?**

Technically, any ESOP transaction or allocation should be at the current appraised value, meaning companies should try to time their ESOP activity with the appraiser's report (buying shares when the report is issued and the trustee determines it is fair market value). In practice, this may be impractical in some cases. There are a few ways to deal with this. If the issue is allocating stock, the allocation can be back-dated to the determination of value. For instance, imagine the plan year ends in December, as does the fiscal year, and that the valuation is completed March 15. The company can make the allocation in March, but credit people's accounts as if it had been made in December at the value that applied to December 31.

If the issue involves a purchase, and the valuation is more than a few weeks old (there is no precise time period), then the trustee should at least certify that there are no material changes in the company or its markets that would cause the ESOP to pay more for the stock than it is currently worth. If the valuation is too conservative, and the ESOP pays less, that is not normally a problem, at least as far as ERISA is concerned. This trustee opinion may require a brief analysis by the appraiser. If conditions have changed materially, however, a new appraisal will be needed.

VALUATION DISCOUNTS

10. What are a lack of control discount and a control premium?

A control premium is simply the mirror image of a lack of control discount. A shareholder owning less than controlling interest in a company has an investment worth less than a shareholder owning a controlling interest. Controlling shareholders can use the assets much more freely, selling them to other buyers, taking larger or smaller dividends, selecting the strategic direction of the company, etc. In takeover battles in public firms, the run-up in price when an offer is made is usually simply a function of someone offering to pay a premium for control.

11. Does control simply mean 50.1% of the stock?

Owning a majority of the stock is one level of control, but some issues in companies require more than a majority vote, so shareholders owning enough to block a transaction, but not enough to exercise day-to-day control, may pay a premium for this lower level of control, although not as high a premium as they would pay for majority control. Similarly, an additional premium would be paid for owning enough stock to control all issues.

Just owning shares is not enough, however. Valuation guidelines for ESOPs say that for the ESOP to pay a control premium, the trust must have control in fact. While this has never been defined in any useful way, it would clearly exclude a situation where the ESOP trustee was controlled by another shareholder. The trustee in that case only has nominal control and should not pay a premium for it.

12. How much is the control premium worth?

There is no simple answer to this. Control premiums are often in the range of 25% to 35%, but can be higher or lower depending on the level of control involved and how valuable that control is given the assets involved. For instance, a company whose assets are encumbered by long-term covenants (such as with lenders, courts or regulatory agencies) would have a lower control premium than a company whose assets are not. There is also a lot of variation from one appraisal firm to another.

13. If the ESOP already has control, does it pay a control price for additional shares?

In most cases, there is an agreement that it will, and if the value is used consistently for all ESOP transactions, including repurchases of shares from employees, this is usually acceptable. Again, however, different appraisers have different philosophies.

14. Can an ESOP pay a control premium if it owns a minority position but plans to acquire a control position later?

There is no consensus on this. Many valuation consultants say an ESOP can pay a control premium if it has a specific option to buy control in a reasonable time, usually three to five years or less, and obtains an irrevocable proxy to vote a sufficient number of additional shares to take over voting control. Others argue this should not be the case; the ESOP should only pay for control when it acquires it. There is no right or wrong approach, but the valuation process should, in any event, use the same assumptions year after year about control.

15. What is the discount for lack of marketability?

Owners of shares in closely held firms cannot sell their shares as easily as owners of publicly traded ones. Because of that, their shares are worth less. Marketability discounts vary considerably, but typically range from 10% to 30% in ESOP transactions. Again, the variation is explained by the particular facts (Are there other potential buyers? Is the ESOP a reliable buyer able to make the payments needed to make the purchase?) and differing appraisal philosophies.

13

CORPORATE GOVERNANCE (CONTROL) IN ESOP COMPANIES

*O*ne of the first questions I get from business owners considering an ESOP is: "Will my employees control the company if I establish an ESOP?" The answer is straightforward: "No!" Very few companies would implement an ESOP if it meant that their company would be controlled by their employees.

The Q&As that follow address the issue of control in ESOP companies.

OVERVIEW

1.   How is it decided who actually has control in an ESOP?

In a publicly traded company, the board of directors is elected by all the shareholders and is responsible for the hiring and firing of management. Employees in a public company ESOP can vote their allocated shares just like any other shareholder. In some public companies, they can direct the voting of unallocated shares as well. In practice, however, employees rarely use the vote any more actively than do other individual shareholders, meaning an ESOP has little or no impact on day-to-day operations of the company or the composition of its board.

In a closely held company, there is more variation. In the most common scenario, employees have only limited voting rights (see Q&A 3), and these do not include voting for the board. Instead, the trustee exercises voting rights. Typically, the trustee is selected by either the board of directors or management. The trustee can be anyone, but is usually either a corporate officer or, in larger companies, an outsider, such as a bank. The trustee, in turn, votes the ESOP shares for the election of the board. Usually, the trustee acts according to directions from the ESOP Committee. The Committee is usually appointed by management or the board and is made up of company officers. This circular arrangement means, in effect, that management and/or the board (and these are often the same people) control the company in much the same way it did prior to the ESOP. Of course, whoever acts as an ESOP's fiduciary (that is, whoever makes decisions for the plan) is legally responsible to make those interests in the best interests of plan participants.

While companies have the discretion to set up the plan this way, more and more plans provide for greater employee involvement. For instance, there may be non-management employee representation on the ESOP Committee. Employees may be given full voting rights on their shares. Employees may also elect one or more representatives to the board. Companies have found that this higher level of employee involvement is usually a plus for the company and very rarely results in significant policy changes other than ones on which there is consensus among the management group as well.

2. Who controls an ESOP?

The ESOP is governed by a trustee who must act for the exclusive benefit of participants. In closely held firms, employees must be able to direct the trustee as to the voting of the shares only on very limited issues; in publicly traded firms, votes pass through on all shareholder issues.

VOTING ESOP SHARES

3. **Who actually votes the ESOP shares?**

    The plan's trustee generally votes all the shares in the ESOP, whether allocated or not. The plan document indicates how the trustee decides how to vote. In closely held companies, the trustee must follow participant directions on allocated shares on several major corporate issues (sale, liquidation, sale of all or substantially all the assets, recapitalization, merger and related issues), but does not have to solicit instructions on voting for the board, agreeing to tender the stock or selling the stock, among other issues.

    In publicly traded companies, trustees must follow participant directions on allocated shares on all issues presented for a shareholder vote. Otherwise, the trustee usually follows the directions of management, the plan committee or another entity specified. While this usually causes no problems, the trustee, or the person(s) directing the trustee, is still responsible to act in the best interests of plan participants.

    Note that while the law requires trustees to solicit employee instructions on specified issues, the trustee has a higher legal obligation under ERISA to override these instructions if they are contrary to the law or plan documents. Such an action would be very rare and would need compelling justification, however.

4. **Who can serve as trustee?**

    Anyone can serve as trustee.

5. **Who typically serves as trustee?**

    The trustee is normally an outside institution with trust experience – most commonly a bank or trust company – an officer of the company or a trust committee usually made up of officers and/or employee representatives.

6. **Who should not be trustee?**

Clearly, the trustee should not be someone without a good working knowledge of the law and the plan. If an insider is chosen, it should not be someone selling stock to the plan. Although this often happens, that person is in too strong a conflict of interest position for this to be appropriate. The trustee should be negotiating for the best deal for participants. Sellers cannot realistically argue for both sides of the transaction.

7. **Who selects the trustee?**

In most cases, management or the board selects the trustee, but, occasionally, an employee committee will make the choice, or, more rarely, outside advisors, investors or creditors may either choose a trustee or approve a trustee. There are no legal requirements for who selects the trustee.

8. **What are the arguments against having an outside trustee?**

Trust services can be very costly (see Q&A 11) and, of course, the very independence of the trustee could diminish insider control in critical circumstances.

9. **What are the arguments for having an outside trustee?**

Assuming the trustee does act as the fiduciary, having an independent, outside trustee provides some protection should the plan's operations be challenged. Presumably, the trustee in this circumstance will make an independent decision not subject to the conflict of interest an insider would face.

10. **Can an independent trustee be designated for a particular issue?**

Yes. A reasonable compromise for many companies is to have an inside trustee or trust committee for normal operations, but appoint an outside trustee for special circumstances that present strong conflicts of interest, such as an acquisition proposal.

11. How much does an outside trustee cost?

That depends on the size and complexity of the plan. Trust services can run anywhere from several thousand dollars per year to hundreds of thousands. The trustee's cost has two components: the time they spend acting as an advisor to the plan committee and an overseer of the plan and the risk the trustee takes of being sued. This latter element may often constitute the larger part of the cost.

12. Should a company select a directed trustee?

Directed trustees do not relieve the plan committee of fiduciary exposure; they are basically custodians to operate the plan. This service comes at a high price, however, and I do not recommend it. The plan can be administered by a plan administrator.

VOTING PASS-THROUGH TO PARTICIPANTS

13. The law requires employees to be able to vote on recapitalizations. What does this mean?

Recapitalization is defined by state corporate statutes, so it can vary from state to state. Generally, it means a change in the number of authorized shares, or the relative rights and preferences of those shares. A small increase in the number of shares may not qualify as a recapitalization. Similarly, many companies already have authorized but unissued shares they can use for various financing purposes (such as selling an ownership stake to an investor or making contributions to the ESOP). Going public would usually be a recapitalization, but refinancing loans would generally not be. If the state statutes require that shareholders be able to vote on an issue as a recapitalization issue, the vote on this must be passed through to ESOP participants.

14. When do employees get to vote on selling a company?

The sale of a company is not necessarily an issue that requires an employee vote. The sale of the assets of a company is, but the sale of stock generally would not be, and certainly would not be if the company's stock were exchanged for stock in an acquiring firm, other than through a merger. State law again would define whether the sale is a matter that requires a shareholder vote, in which case the vote would be passed through to employees.

15. Can ESOPs be structured so employees vote other than one share/ one vote?

There are two ways to do this. First, in closely held companies, the law allows an ESOP to pass through voting on a one person/one vote basis. In some cases, however, other voting arrangements are desired, such as giving some employees more votes than others in a manner unrelated to their share ownership.

In closely held companies there are a limited number of pass-through issues including the sale of all or substantially all of the company's assets, recapitalization, merger or consolidation, liquidation, dissolution and similar issues, but not elections of the board and the sale of stock, among others. In these situations, employees must be allowed to vote their allocated shares according to how many shares they own or one person/one vote. For unallocated shares or for issues for which there is no required pass-through, the trustee can be directed to vote the shares in whatever way the plan is written to dictate.

For instance, a company might hold an employee vote allowing all employees (participants in the plan or not) the right to vote, or it might have an employee vote in which some employees' votes would count more than others. The trustee would then vote the ESOP shares in the same manner, either proportionately or winner takes all.

16. Can voting on ESOP shares be limited to vested shares?

On required voting issues, it cannot, but companies can specify that only vested shares have pass-through voting on non-required issues, such as board elections in closely held companies.

17. Aside from the legally required minimum, can employees direct the trustee as to the voting or tendering of the shares held in their accounts in regards to acquisition proposals?

The law here is very unsettled. Many public companies, and some private firms, provide that employees can direct the trustee of the ESOP to vote or tender their allocated shares as directed and their unallocated or undirected shares in the same proportion as the allocated shares. Generally, companies that do this name each participant as a fiduciary for the ESOP shares. The issue here is whether the trustee can simply record the votes or directions or must make an independent judgment.

The most important case on this issue is Reich v. NationsBank. NationsBank acted as trustee for Polaroid's ESOP, which used this mirror voting and tendering approach. As part of a successful effort to block a hostile acquisition bid, Polaroid expanded an existing ESOP, and participants generally sided with management.

The Department of Labor (DOL) sued, saying that the trustee should not simply have followed employee directions on unallocated and undirected shares, although it could follow them on allocated shares. The Department contended that the current participants could not direct the voting of unallocated shares because these would be allocated to unknown future participants. Moreover, the trustee has an affirmative duty under ERISA to make decisions for the exclusive benefit of plan participants, regardless of participant directions. Employees could be named fiduciaries for shares allocated to them, but not for shares that were not. On these other shares, the trustee must make the decision.

In a subsequent letter to the AFL-CIO, however, the DOL took what appears to be a different view, saying that the trustees could only override employee directions on unallocated or undirected shares if there were a compelling reason to do so. Since most acquisitions can present a variety of arguments why different courses of action make sense for shareholders (and the trustees must decide the issue based on employee interests as shareholders, not employees), it could be difficult in many cases for a trustee to override employee directions.

The consensus of legal opinion on this issue seems to be that employees can direct allocated shares, can be named as fiduciaries for all shares and can give directions to the trustee. The trustee, however, should ultimately have the power to make an independent decision if there is, as the DOL puts it, a compelling reason to override the employee directions. For instance, the trustee may override if there is persuasive evidence that both short- and long-term stock values will do better under an offer the employees do not favor. In more ambiguous situations, however, employee directions would probably be acceptable. In any case, the trustees must create a clear paper trail about why the decision was made and why it is consistent with ERISA. Participants must also be given clear, objective information about the competing alternatives, much as any other shareholder would in a proxy battle.

ESOP NON-VOTING STOCK

18. Can an ESOP own non-voting stock?

Yes, typically non-voting preferred stock. But the shares must be convertible into voting shares at the discretion of the trustee.

19. Why would a company choose preferred stock for the ESOP?

It has a more stable value, which may be important to participants. It also can pay a higher dividend than common stock. Because dividends generally do not count towards the 415 limits in C corporation ESOPs, this can allow a company to make larger payments to the ESOP than it could with common. Also, preferred stock usually yields a higher sales price for the seller.

14

DISTRIBUTIONS TO PARTICIPANTS

*E*mployees become entitled to a distribution of the value of their vested ESOP account upon the occurrence of one of the following distributable events:

- Death
- Disability
- Retirement
- Termination of Service

In addition, when an employee reaches age 55 and has participated in the ESOP for 10 years, he becomes entitled to diversify a portion of his ESOP account.

These four distributable events and the diversification rule require that the stock in an employee's account be converted to cash. This legal obligation to convert stock in an ESOP account into cash is referred to as the ESOP "repurchase obligation."

My experience has been that in larger companies (those with at least 100 employees) the repurchase obligation, generally, is not a major financial constraint on the company if the Plan's distribution provisions are properly structured and if the company experiences steady financial performance. However, in other companies, the repurchase obligation may be a significant factor which, if not properly budgeted, could threaten the company's financial health. Therefore, prior to implementing an ESOP, a company should discuss the ESOP distribution provisions and their potential impact on the repurchase obligation with an experienced ESOP consultant.

The Q&As that follow discuss the ESOP distribution rules and the repurchase liability.

OVERVIEW

1. **When does a company have to start distributing an employee's account?**

   If an employee leaves because of death, retirement, disability or reaches retirement age after termination but before an ESOP payout has started, distribution must start during the plan year following the event. Otherwise, distribution must start within six years after the plan year of termination. If there is an outstanding ESOP loan, distribution to terminating employees of a C corporation does not have to start until the loan is repaid. This provision only clearly applies to C corporations.

   There is no logical reason that S corporations should not be able to do this as well, but a literal reading of the law does not allow it. As noted below, this does not apply in the same way to employees receiving distributions because of death or retirement. Distributions for any 5% owners must begin not later than April 1 following the calendar year in which a participant reaches age 70½. Once the distribution commences, it can be paid out in a lump sum or in equal installments, with interest, over a period not exceeding five years (or more for balances over $985,000 as of 2009, indexed annually for inflation).

2. **Under what circumstances is the company permitted to distribute account balances under $5,001 to terminated employees earlier than five years following termination?**

   Many ESOPs are written to allow companies flexibility in the timing of distributions of small account balances, and some companies with plans that do not offer this flexibility are choosing to amend their plans. For plans that do allow such flexibility, the ESOP administration committee (or parallel body) can make distributions earlier than the five years, provided that (a) there is a written distribution policy, (b) the acceleration is not done in a way that discriminates in favor of highly compensated employees and (c) the acceleration does not favor one class of employees over another.

The rules vary depending on the size of the account balance to be distributed. For accounts under $1,001, the company can distribute in cash without obtaining the beneficiary's consent. For amounts greater than $1,000 but under $5,001, the company is required to roll the distribution into an IRA, unless the participant elects otherwise.

Given all this, most plan sponsors choose among three options:
1. Automatically distribute all amounts under $5,001 without obtaining participant consent
2. Require participant consent for all distributions (even those under $5,001)
3. Require consent for distributions over $1,000 and under $5,001; distribute amounts under $1,001 without obtaining consent.

3. **A company can defer the start of its ESOP distributions until after its loan is repaid. Does this even apply to distributions due to death, retirement or disability?**
   - In cases of death, for shares on which the loan has not yet been repaid, distribution does not have to start right away, but must be completed by the end of the calendar year of the fifth anniversary after death and made to the beneficiary, regardless of the loan status.

- For retirement, for people who are not 5% owners, distribution must start no later than the 60th day after the end of the plan year in which the later of these events occur:
  1. The participant reaches age 65 or, if earlier, the plan's normal retirement age.
  2. The employee reaches age 70½ and is a 5% or more owner, the calendar year in which the employee retires; or
  3. The 10th anniversary of participation in the plan.

(Note: These are general qualified plan rules that apply to all aspects of ESOP distributions, not just the deferral of distributions until after the loan is repaid.)

This means that employees who reach age 65 prior to 10 years from the anniversary date of their original participation in the plan could have to wait until the 10th anniversary occurs to become eligible. (Note this is not 10 years service, but 10 years from the start of participation.) Plan participation would include years in a predecessor defined contribution plan if it was not terminated, but rather folded into the ESOP.

While this delay is allowed by the law, that does not mean it will be in the plan document. Many plan documents provide for earlier payouts for retirees. Alternatively, many other plans provide for the maximum legal flexibility but, in practice, pay out sooner. From an employee relations standpoint, not to mention the need of employees for retirement income, this earlier distribution policy normally makes sense.

4. **If an ESOP loan is refinanced, can the extension of the loan period further extend the time the employer is allowed before paying distributions to participants?**

Yes. ESOP sponsors with a leveraged plan can generally delay distribution until after a loan is repaid. Refinancing could extend the term of the loan and hence the time for repayment.

5. **When an ESOP delays distribution until after the loan is repaid, and pays in installments at that point, can participants still receive a five-year installment payout?**

It depends on the circumstances. If an employee leaves prior to the payment of the loan, and would be due to have distribution completed prior to the loan being paid, then payment must be completed in the first year after the loan is repaid.

If a participant would have had all the payments completed between the final payment on the loan and the end of the five-year period after the loan is repaid, then payment can start after the loan is repaid, but must be completed by the time the last installment would normally have been paid.

If the participant leaves before the loan is repaid, and was not due to have the distribution completed until five years after the final loan payment, then the five-year period would be tacked on. Examples make this clearer:

- Participant A terminates in 1998 and, under the plan, should receive installment payments starting in 2000 and concluding in 2005. But an ESOP loan will not be repaid until 2006. This participant must be paid in full in 2006.
- Participant B terminates in 1998. But for the fact that the loan has not been repaid, B would normally have payment commence in 2000, and would be paid in six installments through 2005. The loan is not repaid until 2003, however. B

must start to receive payments in 2003 and have all payments made by 2005. While the law is not clear, B should probably receive the equivalent of four installment payments in 2003 and the remaining two payments in each year thereafter.

- Participant C terminates in 1998. The plan provides that distribution will not begin until 2002. The loan will be repaid in 2001. In this case, the payment of the loan precedes the start of distribution, so does not affect the operation of the plan rules on installment payouts.

Note that each of these cases assumes the employee leaves for reasons other than retirement or death, the rules for which are explained in a prior question.

6.   When an employee puts shares to the company, does the company have to pay for them all at once?

No. The company can pay out in equal annual installments, with adequate interest (a market rate) over a period not exceeding five years. For distributions over $985,000 (in 2009 dollars), the payout can be extended another year for each additional $195,000 (in 2009 dollars). The promise must be backed by adequate security. A promise to pay based on the full faith and credit of the company is not enough.

7.   If a valuation is not completed until months after the distribution date, should the company pay interest on the distribution amount?

While a company could do this, most practitioners agree that the law does not require it, although there is no clear legal guidance on this.

8.   If a partially vested employee leaves with an account partly in leveraged ESOP shares and partly in other investments, is there an order to paying out the account?

The law says that leveraged shares are forfeited last. What this means is that the ESOP first pays out all of whatever is in the other investment account to cover the vested portion of the total account balance. If that is not enough, then the ESOP starts using the leveraged shares. So assume an employee has $20,000 in an ESOP account, of which 40% is an other investment account. The employee is 50% vested. Of the $10,000 due the employee, $8,000 comes from the other investment account and $2,000 from leveraged shares.

9. **Can early distributions be made in the case of hardships?**
An ESOP or other qualified plan can make in-service distributions prior to normal distribution periods for hardships or for vested benefits that have been in the plan at least two years. Hardships are defined as situations necessary to meet an immediate and heavy financial need that can only be satisfied by the withdrawal. Certain conditions meet a safe harbor test for hardship, including medical expenses for the participant or participant's family, purchase of a principal residence, payment of educational expenses or payments necessary to avoid eviction from a principal residence. Otherwise, the plan must provide for a facts and circumstances test that is subject to IRS review.

Early distributions are, in any event, subject to a 10% excise tax, plus additional taxes that would apply to the distribution if it were not an early distribution.

10. **If a valuation is not completed for some months after the end of the plan year, how should the company handle distributions in terms of the price it pays for shares to make sure the price reflects fair market value? The law says the distribution must be at fair market value, but given the lag between the end of the plan year triggering a distribution option and the valuation, things can change.**
First, plan language should be clear that distributions will occur as soon as practicable after the required time from termination, retirement, death or disability. That recognizes that it is not possible

to pay out as of the actual date of the current valuation.

Assume the valuation is completed six months after the end of the plan year. If your policy says that an employee can choose a distribution prior to that date, the plan would normally say the price of the shares would be the most recent valuation (the one completed in the prior June). But employees could also wait until the new valuation is completed and then be paid within a short (30 days, for instance) window. If employees leave after the valuation date, but before the end of the plan year, they would get the June 30 price.

Alternatively, the company could simply say that all distributions will occur within 30 days of the completion of the June 30 valuation. If a company wanted to provide for potential hardship issues, or for death or retirement, it could allow employees to take a percentage of the distribution (such as 75%) and then be trued-up at the June 30 date. That way, the company is protected if the stock value drops sharply from the prior valuation.

11. What are the options for distributions of an ESOP account in shares?

Stock distributions can be made in a lump sum or in installments. Non-lump sum distributions are subject to income tax and a 10% penalty if received before death, retirement at or after age 55, age 59½ or disability. If the payments are in installments, the company must buy back the shares at the employee's option within 30 days of their distribution. If the stock is distributed in a lump sum, and the company is not public, the repurchase can be paid for immediately in cash or over up to five years with adequate security and interest (see Q&A 15).

12. Can a company require employees to take cash instead of shares?

Not unless (1) either (a) company by-laws specify that all or substantially all the stock in the company be owned by employees or (b) the company is an S corporation, and (2) the plan document specifies that the company can offer the cash value of accounts instead. If the company is a bank and has a cash only provision, it can also choose not to offer employees shares when they leave.

13. Can a participant demand that part of a distribution be in cash and part in stock?

Yes, unless (1) either (a) company by-laws specify that all or substantially all the stock in the company be owned by employees or (b) the company is an S corporation, and (2) the plan document specifies that the company can offer the cash value of accounts instead. If the company is a bank and has a cash only provision, it can also choose not to offer employees shares when they leave.

14. If an employee has both a stock and cash account, does the participant still have the right to demand stock for the cash account when receiving a distribution?

Yes, unless company by-laws specify that all or substantially all the stock in the company be owned by employees and the plan document specifies that the company can offer the cash value of accounts instead, or the company is a bank and has a cash only provision.

15. What is adequate security?

Adequate security must be something tangible, such as a hard asset, accounts payable, a letter of credit, money in the bank, a bond or other insurance.

16. **Can assets of former participants be segregated and held in cash rather than company stock? If they can, do the accounts actually have to have cash or cash equivalents in them, or can dollar amounts just be credited to them?**

It can be held in cash or cash equivalents, but the trustee needs to do so in a prudent and non-discriminatory way, and the trustee has a fiduciary obligation to ensure that the money is available when the distribution is set to begin. For instance, say the company has a five-year waiting period before distribution begins. An employee leaves the company, and the ESOP administrator calculates that the employee's vested account balance is worth $50,000. The plan can invest the cash equivalent of the value in other investments until the distribution begins.

Some plans have provisions saying that the plan only is obligated to come up with an equivalent amount, but does not actually have to make the investment. Treasury officials have told ESOP practitioners informally that this is not allowable.

EMPLOYEE TAXATION ON ESOP DISTRIBUTIONS

17. **What is the employee's tax liability for ESOP distributions?**

If the employee puts the money into an IRA or the distribution is rolled forward into another qualified plan in another company, there is no tax liability when the money is withdrawn. The withdrawal is taxed as ordinary income. Otherwise, the employee must pay ordinary income tax on the value of company contributions to the plan, capital gains taxes on the appreciation in share value when sold (this only applies to lump-sum distributions), and a 10% penalty if the distribution is not after age 59½ or for death, termination after age 55 or disability. For capital gains holding period requirement purposes, the time the shares have been in the employee's account does count.

The rollover to an IRA or another qualified plan is normally done as a direct rollover, meaning the employee notifies the company that the account should be rolled over into the successor plan before the account is paid out. Alternatively, the amount can be paid out to the employee who then has 60 days to roll it into an IRA. However, in making this choice, companies need to consider the possible impact of withholding plan rules. For details on this, see Q&A 20 on Withholding Rules.

18. If a company makes a distribution to an employee by providing a note and making installment payments on it, can the employee roll the amount over into an IRA?

Technically, when a participant receives a distribution of shares that are repurchased with a note, he or she has a taxable event for the full amount of the distribution (setting aside possible capital gains treatment on the net unrealized appreciation, which is another issue). So, since the payments that follow are related to amounts already taxed as a distribution, they are not eligible for a roll-over. The only way to properly accomplish a rollover where stock is distributed and a note is used for a repurchase is to have the stock distributed to an IRA (and there are trustees who will accept the stock or a stock power as rollover assets) and then have the trustee of the IRA sell the shares to the company and accept the note. You might argue that the note is the proceeds of the sale of the securities which would allow it to be rolled over itself during the 60-day period after the distribution is made. The best arguments we've heard are that the note itself does not represent proceeds of the sale and, therefore, it is not eligible to be rolled over at all.

19. **If an employee leaving for reasons other than death, disability or retirement receives a lump-sum distribution that is paid in installments, with interest, what is the tax treatment if it is not rolled into an IRA?**

The cost basis of the shares is taxed in the year of distribution at ordinary income rates, plus a 10% penalty. The appreciation on the shares is taxed at capital gains rates, but is paid ratably with each installment payment. Interest on the remaining balance is taxed each year as ordinary income.

20. **Is there a company withholding issue on the stock?**

If an employee does not consent to have the distribution rolled over into an IRA or a successor benefit plan at another company, the ESOP sponsor must withhold 20% for federal income tax purposes. This withholding, however, is reduced to the extent the distribution is in stock. If all the distribution is in company stock, there is no withholding. If it is not, funds must be withheld to the extent there is cash, up to 20%. For instance, if 10% of the distribution is in cash, 10% is withheld. There may also be separate state withholding rules.

21. **If an employee leaving before death, retirement or disability receives a distribution of shares and chooses not to roll it into an IRA, is the entire distribution subject to the 10% early withdrawal penalty?**

Only the part of the distribution attributable to the corporate contribution is subject to the 10% penalty; the remainder is treated as net unrealized appreciation and is taxed as a capital gain.

22. **Are corporate contributions to an ESOP subject to FICA?**

Corporate contributions to retirement plans are not subject to FICA (Federal Insurance Contributions Act, the law that governs contributions to Social Security). Employee contributions, however, are subject to FICA.

23. Can an employee get net unrealized appreciation tax treatment on S ESOP share distributions?

There is nothing in the law to prevent this, but it may not be of much value. First, companies may be reluctant to distribute actual shares to employees for fear they will violate the 100 shareholder rule of S corporations, or simply because they don't want shares held outside the company. As an S ESOP, they don't have to provide a stock distribution. Second, in an S corporation, the owner's basis is adjusted upward every time a distribution is made. Therefore, when the employee gets the shares, the basis is often very high relative to the value received, thus making most of the distribution subject to ordinary income tax and, possibly, a penalty tax.

24. How does the company determine the net unrealized appreciation on participant accounts?

For each allocation, the recordkeeper for the plan must post the cost basis for the shares allocated to the participant's account. If the plan simply receives annual cash contributions to buy shares, or just shares themselves, then the cost basis is the value of the shares when allocated. If the plan is a leveraged ESOP, the cost basis, no matter when allocated, is how much the plan paid for the shares. If the allocations are from forfeitures, the original cost basis of the shares applies. If the allocations are from the repurchase of shares from departing employees, the cost basis is the price at which they were repurchased. These various numbers are then averaged to create a running average cost basis for the shares.

25. If an employee's lump-sum distribution from an ESOP is paid with a note, how is it taxed?

The employee must pay tax on the distribution at the time of distribution. This includes ordinary income tax on the basis of the contributions, net unrealized appreciation treatment for the appreciation on the stock and the 10% penalty for early distributions, if applicable.

The net unrealized appreciation arguably could be recognized ratably as the note is paid and thus taxed as a capital gain. If possible, it is better to roll the note into an IRA, but it may not be easy to find an IRA trustee willing to accept this kind of security.

26. If an employee takes a distribution in stock intending to hold onto it and sell later to benefit from net unrealized appreciation tax treatment, but then decides to roll the money into an IRA, what happens?

If the employee decides to roll over the amount within 60 days of distribution, it can be rolled into an IRA. The cost basis of the shares would already have been taxed as ordinary income (through withholding), however, and could only be returned later through a refund when the employee fills out his tax returns. The employee can roll up to the entire amount of the distribution into the ESOP, assuming the employee has the cash to do so.

DIVERSIFICATION OF ESOP SHARES

27. Are all ESOP shares subject to diversification?

No. Securities acquired before January 1, 1987, are not covered, with a few technical exceptions. These shares are subject to tracking if they are subsequently repurchased by the ESOP and re-contributed to the ESOP (that is, they are still not subject to diversification rules). Also, company stock account balances worth under $500 do not have to be diversified.

28. How can the ESOP account be diversified?

The ESOP can pay out the benefit to the employee, which if it's in stock, the employee can put back to the company under its normal put rules. Alternatively, the distribution can be transferred into another qualified plan with at least three investment options, or the ESOP itself can offer three options.

29. How do most companies diversify?

Most privately held firms diversify by paying the account to the participant; most public firms have other plans accomplish the diversification.

30. How much of the ESOP account may be diversified?

25% at age 55 and each year thereafter and 50% at age 60. This is cumulative; an employee diversifying 25% at age 55 cannot diversify 50% of the remainder at 60.

At the end of each plan year, for the six years starting in the year in which the employee becomes eligible, the employee must have 90 days to choose whether to diversify, and the company has 180 days to accomplish the diversification. At the end of the six years, no further right applies. In other words, an employee might choose not to diversify in the first year, then diversify 20% in the second and 5% more in the third. Another employee might not reach 10 years of service until age 58 was reached. That employee can diversify up to 25% in the first year and, cumulatively, up to 25% until age 63 is reached, at which point up to 50% could be diversified. There is a caveat here, however. The first diversification election occurs at the year the employee is over 55 and has 10 years of service. At that point, the employee can diversify up to 25% for the next five years and 50% in the sixth election year, even if this occurs after age 60.

The complexity comes in between years one and five. The number of shares eligible to be diversified is 25% of the total number of shares added to the account since the plan's inception (or for shares acquired after December 31, 1986, if companies have such shares and account for them separately), minus any shares already diversified. In other words, the number is 25% of the starting eligible share account balance plus 25% of any incremental share contributions in subsequent years minus the number of shares already diversified.

For instance, say on year one of diversification there are 1,000 shares. Then:

> Year one: 1,000 shares in account
> Diversification right: 250 shares

> Year two: 750 shares in account, plus 100 additional shares contributed in year two now subject to diversification.

So, the calculation for year two is:
1,000 shares plus 100 shares since year one in the account. So now the calculation is 25% of 1,110 shares, or 275 shares eligible to be diversified; however, 250 shares were already diversified. Therefore, only 25 more shares can be diversified.

This is the same as just taking 25% of the newly allocated shares and letting the employee diversify that amount. Where it is different is where the employee diversified less than 25% in year one. For instance, say the employee has 1,000 shares in the first year of diversification and chooses to diversify 200. In year two, 100 more shares are added. So now the calculation is:

> 1,100 total allocated shares x. 25 = 275 shares.
> - 200 shares already diversified

So an additional 75 shares can be diversified, not 25, as would be the case if only the new 100 allocated shares were counted. The key idea here is that diversification is based on the cumulative number of shares allocated in any year.

31. How long does the diversification option remain in effect?

Generally, the participant becomes eligible on the first day of the plan year following the end of the plan year in which the participant has reached age 55 and has completed 10 years of participation in the plan. At that point, the participant has 90 days to decide whether to diversify. For each of the next four years, at the start of the plan year, the employee has an additional 90-day period to elect to diversify.

32. If an ESOP participant chooses to diversify in a particular year, how much can be diversified in subsequent years?

The diversification option applies to whatever is in the account in any year at age 55 and after 10 years of plan service (or sooner if a company so chooses). The participant has the right to diversify up to 25% of plan assets invested in stock in each year between ages 55 and 60 and 50% for each year at 60 and beyond. For instance, if an employee chooses to diversify 25% at age 55, and continues to receive allocations of company stock thereafter, each year the participant can diversify up to 25% of these additional stock distributions. If a participant initially chose to diversify less than 25% or 50%, that participant could diversify an additional amount such that at the time of the election, the total stock diversification would equal 25% or 50%.

33. Do diversification election rules apply to small account balances?

If the participant has less than $500 in the fair market value of employer shares on the date of the election period, then the company does not have to offer a diversification election.

34. Does the diversification election apply only to company stock in the account?

Yes. If an account is 75% stock, for instance, the employee can diversify 25% of that 75% in the first year of eligibility. The fact that the account is already 25% diversified does not satisfy the diversification requirement.

35. Can a participant choose to revoke a diversification election?

During the 90-day period, participants can change their minds; after that, they cannot move assets back into company stock.

36. Can an ESOP provide more than the legally required diversification?

Yes. The ESOP can allow up to any amount to be diversified at any age. Any amounts above what is required, however, remain subject to the participant's subsequent right to demand their payout in company stock, unless the participant's right to diversification is satisfied by paying out people directly. Participants would rarely make this demand, but this does add some complication to plan administration.

37. What are the diversification requirements if someone attains age 55 and 10 years of service after termination of employment but while still a plan participant (because distributions do not occur for some years after termination)? What if they have 10 years of service, but are not 55 when they are terminated? Would they be eligible to diversify when they reach 55 if they have not received a distribution?

First, your plan document should spell out what to do in these situations. There is no regulatory guidance on this, and the statute is ambiguous. The consensus is that in the first case, the employee would not qualify for diversification because he or she would not meet the 10-year rule, which the consensus interprets as years when an employee would be eligible for an allocation. The second scenario is also not entirely clear, but the employee probably should be allowed to diversify.

38. What are the tax consequences to the participant of diversification?

If the diversification occurs internally, there are none. If the account is paid out, the participant can defer taxation by rolling the amount in an IRA. Thus, the distribution is treated in the same way as a lump-sum distribution in the case of an employee leaving the company. If not rolled into an IRA, the amount is taxable as ordinary income. There will also be a 10% excise tax if the participant is under age 59½ and has not left the company, or the participant left the company before the calendar year in which the participant turned 55 and does not roll over the distribution. For details on withholding rules and distribution options and consequences for employees, see Q&As 17-26.

39. What is the obligation of the company to notify the participant of the diversification option?

Once a participant becomes eligible, the company must provide the employee with a description of the options in writing.

40. When can a participant make the diversification election?

The election would normally occur during a 90-day period after the end of the close of each plan year in which the participant is qualified to make the election. The company then has to make the diversification within 90 days following the end of this 90-day election period.

41. When do you need a valuation done to use for a distribution from a diversification election?

You can use the most recent valuation if your plan specifies this, although it is preferable to time your diversification election to occur just once a year, being completed not more than 90 days after the close of the plan year. That way, the valuation will be fairly recent.

42. Who is required to be eligible to diversify holdings in an ESOP account?

Anyone with 10 years or more of participation in the plan (defined as the ESOP or a predecessor plan whose assets were transferred to the ESOP) and who is 55 years or older. The diversification option applies only to shares acquired after 1986, however.

43. Why would a company want to go beyond the legal minimum for diversification?

There could be a number of reasons. Most commonly, it could make the plan more appealing to employees (especially in those plans where employee funds are used to purchase some or all shares), or it could reduce repurchase obligations in companies with rapidly increasing stock values.

HANDLING ESOP REPURCHASE OBLIGATIONS

44. Are ESOP repurchases typically in lump sums or installments?

Other than for small accounts (typically $5,000 or less), just under half are in lump sums; the rest are in installments. Small accounts are almost always paid in a lump sum.

45. Are repurchased shares reallocated immediately?

Yes, shares repurchased through the ESOP would normally be reallocated immediately. If you want to reallocate them on a different schedule, the company should buy back the shares and then re-contribute them.

46. Can a company transfer an employee's stock balance into cash after termination but before distribution?

1. It can, but it must be done in accordance with a specific policy. For instance, the plan document or distribution policy could provide:

- that vested balances of X dollars are distributable after the end of the year following a participant's date of termination, and
- that vested balances in excess of X dollars shall be converted to cash as of the end of the plan year following the date of termination and invested in a separate interest bearing account which the trustee shall establish on behalf of each participant.

2. The actual cash must be invested. Some practitioners have argued that accounts simply representing the amount are permissible. An IRS representative has informally stated at The ESOP Association's National Conference that they do not believe this is allowable. The segregated account, including earnings, is distributable then after a specified number of years. (Note: It may be necessary to offer the former participant the option of having this account converted to shares at the time of the actual distribution.)

Another alternative, if planned for in advance, would be to convert the former employee's balance to preferred stock with a stated dividend rate payable in additional shares of the preferred stock. Under this alternative, the distribution to the employee is delayed as is the company's repurchase obligation.

47. Does it make sense for companies to borrow money to fund repurchase obligations?

One strategy used to repurchase stock is to borrow funds, either through the ESOP or the company, to buy stock from departing employees when they leave. If the ESOP is repurchasing the stock, the stock must be distributed to the participant and then repurchased using the borrowed funds. If the after-tax cost of the money is lower than the rate of growth in the stock value over whatever delay period the company otherwise would have imposed, then the strategy is a net gainer for the company.

48. How can we assess how much the repurchase obligation will be?

A repurchase obligation study assesses this issue. It should be done by professionals or with their advice, and should be updated periodically.

We include a sample repurchase obligation study in our online appendix (www.esopcoach.com).

49. How do most companies handle ESOP repurchase obligations?

A 1999 NCEO (National Center for Employee Ownership) survey found that 45% of the companies fund repurchase obligations primarily out of cash flow, 47% out of contributions to the ESOP, and 8% with life insurance or other means. Companies that use cash flow to repurchase stock almost always then re-contribute the stock to the ESOP.

50. How does the repurchase obligation affect value?

There are two issues here. First there is the issue of whether the put option (the requirement that the employee can sell the stock back to the company for its fair market value) itself affects value. The second is whether the cash flow needed to fund repurchase reduces value.

Some appraisers argue that the put option in an ESOP reduces or eliminates the marketability discount. Others argue it depends on the plan's proven ability to repurchase shares. Still others say it depends on whether the contributions to the ESOP needed to repurchase shares increase or decrease what the company would otherwise spend on benefit plans. Some appraisers contend that the put option is not the same thing as a liquid market and should provide only a small reduction in the marketability discount. Passionate arguments are made on all sides.

The NCEO has taken a position on this, namely that the put option itself does not create a market unless the company shows it has (or can contribute to the ESOP) the funds to satisfy the put. If that is the case, however, the commitment of these funds to a non-productive purpose should reduce the company's value unless they constitute no more than what would be contributed to employee benefits plans if the ESOP were not in place. Even then, some marketability discount should remain, because the put option is a restricted right to sell shares, subject to all the rules, delays and limits of the ESOP distribution formula.

Many people disagree with this, however, arguing, for instance, that the company could always sell or, in some cases, go public to provide liquidity, or that not to pay the highest price possible is unfair to current participants.

Almost everyone agrees that there is a tendency in valuations to make favorable assumptions up front (such as assuming the put eliminates the marketability discount) to provide sellers a high price. Trustees need to be very wary of this, however, because it can harm the interests of plan participants down the road.

The second issue is how cash flow requirements for the repurchase affect value. All private companies have a repurchase obligation; the ESOP does not create a new issue here. The ESOP is also a form of compensation, however. If a company contributes cash to the ESOP to buy back shares or buys shares and re-contributes them to the ESOP, it is using tax-deductible dollars to fund its repurchase (which, remember, exists no matter who owns the stock), arguably making the ESOP repurchase favorable relative to other private company requirements. If the amount being contributed is equal to or less than what would otherwise be contributed to employee benefit plans, then the ESOP repurchase has a positive or neutral effect on value; if it is greater, it should reduce value to the extent the higher contributions are not offset by the tax benefits associated with the contribution or additional productivity the additional contributions might generate.

51. What are the advantages and disadvantages of delaying repurchase obligations?

Obviously, delaying the repurchase conserves company cash but, assuming the former participants' account balances remain in company stock, it also means people no longer with the firm benefit from its growth. If the company's stock value increases faster than alternative investments the company might make, or the company's after-tax cost of money, then delaying the repurchase can simply mean what is owed to employees grows faster than the company's ability to pay. On the other hand, delaying distributions can be important if employees who have large account balances are tempted to leave the company to cash in their accounts.

52. What is the cost basis of repurchased shares?

The cost basis of reallocated shares bought by the ESOP is the price at which they were repurchased.

53. When an ESOP repurchases shares from departing employees, does this have an impact on Section 415 (individual annual addition) or Section 404 (corporate deduction) limits?

If the ESOP uses its own existing cash to buy back shares, then there are no 404 or 415 issues because there are no contributions being made. Cash goes out of employee accounts, where it has already been allocated, and is replaced by shares. If the company contributes additional cash to the ESOP to repurchase shares, then this too is an additional contribution that would affect both 415 and 404.

54. What is Corporate Owned Life Insurance (COLI) and is it a good repurchase strategy?

COLI is life insurance owned by the company on the lives of ESOP participants. The company is the beneficiary should the participant die, with the money then used for the repurchase of shares. Premiums paid on COLI policies are not deductible and the death benefits are received tax-free. Meanwhile, the build up in value in the policy is not taxable to the company. The cash value can be borrowed, but for policies issued after June 8, 1997, interest is not deductible unless the insured person is a key person (limited to between 5 and 20 persons, depending on the size of the company). In that case, the interest on loans of up to $50,000 may be deductible.

Companies follow two typical strategies in using corporate owned life insurance for repurchase. One option is to insure those people whose accounts are expected to become very large. If these people die before termination, the policies can pay all or part of their distributions. If they do not die before termination, the company pays off the participant at termination, but holds on to the policy until the participant does die. At that point, the life insurance proceeds revert to the company. Over time, this can help create cash flow to fund repurchase.

15

THE FUTURE OF ESOPS

*I*n a political and economic environment in which Congress is trying to eliminate as many tax benefits as possible in order to balance the federal budget, I'm often asked, "When will Congress kill ESOPs?" There are many reasons why I believe ESOPs will survive and continue to flourish.

ESOPs have a long history of support by both Republicans and Democrats. Since 1974, Congress has passed over 25 laws promoting ESOPs. There have been only a few instances in which the law has been changed to restrict ESOP benefits. For example, on March 14, 2001, Congress added Section 409(p) to the Internal Revenue Code. This new law, known as the S Corporation ESOP Anti-Abuse Rule, was designed to eliminate a planning scheme that clearly needed to be shut down. Other than that law, Congress has consistently supported the formation of new ESOPs and the expansion of existing ones. And it has worked. Since 1974, 20,000 ESOPs have been created. The total value of all ESOP assets is more than $925 billion and more than 13 million employees (12% of the U. S. workforce) participate in an ESOP.

Certainly the positive contributions ESOPs have made to companies is a factor in my optimistic outlook. It has been conclusively proven by 70 academic studies that employee ownership results in measurable performance improvement for the companies that sponsor the plans and their employees. Companies that share ownership perform better than they did prior to sharing ownership. Employee ownership leads to increased productivity and company profitability. It results in increased sales and employment growth and employee-owned firms survive longer than comparable firms that do not share ownership.

The benefits to employees play another key role. ESOPs provide employees more generous retirement benefits than are provided by traditional retirement plans. Studies indicate that, on average, companies contribute 4% of pay to employees' 401k accounts. By contrast, companies contribute, on average, 10% of pay to employees' ESOP accounts. Employers contribute 250% more to ESOPs in many instances because that is the amount that is required to service the ESOP debt. Making these large contributions accomplishes the dual goals of retiring ESOP debt and providing very rich employee retirement benefits.

Many people would argue that allowing a company the ability to deduct principal payments on ESOP loans is a tax benefit. They say that such a generous tax benefit has no place in the law at a time when we need to focus on balancing the federal budget. In reality, employers' ESOP contributions are actually a form of compensation, since the contributions to employees' accounts will be paid to them, with earnings, when they have a distributable event, such as retirement. Since compensation paid to employees generally is a tax deductible expense, the fact that employers get a tax deduction for ESOP contributions (which the ESOP uses to service debt) is completely consistent with the tax law and should not be viewed as a special tax benefit for ESOPs.

There is also an argument that S corporation ESOPs delay the taxation of a company's income. With an ESOP-owned S corporation, the ESOP's portion of the company's income is not subject to taxation at the time it is earned. Instead, employees will be taxed in the future when the value of their ESOP account is paid to them. At that point they will be taxed not only on the amount of income that was previously deferred but also on productivity gains reflected in the appreciation of their ESOP accounts. Therefore, there is no reduction in tax collections from the S corporation ESOP structure.

If ESOPs do not reduce tax revenues collected by the federal government and if they provide greater retirement benefits to employees than the traditional retirement plans, why would anyone oppose their expansion?

The only possible objection to ESOPs is what is known as the Rescue ESOP. United Airlines, Weirton Steel and The Tribune Company are examples of companies that have used Rescue ESOPs. These plans generally are established for companies that are in desperate financial condition. They often involve wage and benefit concessions by employees and very aggressive/risky financing structures.

Companies that use Rescue ESOPs often wind up in bankruptcy. However, there are a couple of key points worth noting. First, Rescue ESOPs comprise less than 5% of all ESOPs. Second, most of these companies would have failed with or without an ESOP. The ESOP did not cause their failure. The ESOP just failed to save them.

I believe ESOPs will continue to be supported by both political parties and that there is no legislative threat that should make a business owner hesitant to use an ESOP as part of his Ownership Succession Planning. However, even if you do not agree with this premise you should know that if you adopt an ESOP and the tax law later changes, your plan will almost certainly be grandfathered. Congress is loath to make retroactive changes to the tax law, especially when doing so could have dire consequences to the employees who participate in plans.

16

THE ESOP PROCESS

Succession Planning is a process that takes time and the assistance of planning professionals. In this concluding chapter, I will describe how the ESOP planning and implementation process might evolve in a typical scenario.

Owners often have to be jolted into recognizing the need to engage in succession planning. This jolt might come in the form of:

- **A medical crisis.** Many business owners resist recognizing their own mortality and avoid planning until they have a brush with mortality. This may come from a personal experience with cancer or heart disease or from a close friend's medical crisis or untimely death.

- **Defection of a key employee.** When a long-term, trusted employee announces he is leaving the company it can send shock waves through the owner, especially if the key employee was integral to the owner's succession planning. Sometimes the owner can begin the planning process immediately and retain the key employee. However, in many cases it is too late to convince the key employee to stay and the owner has to learn a hard lesson from his mistakes.

- **A third-party demand.** Many times third parties will require business owners to implement a succession plan. I have seen lenders, surety companies, suppliers, customers and franchisors tell business owners to either implement a succession plan or the third party will cut them off. These third parties recognize the risk of their business relationship being disrupted by inadequate succession planning.

Once a business owner recognizes the need to start the planning process, he often will begin discussing it with one of his key advisors. In my experience this, most often, is his CPA. Typically a company's CPA knows the business owner and his company better than any of its other advisors. As the business owner discusses succession planning alternatives with his CPA, the CPA often brings specialists into the discussion – investment bankers, estate and/or transactional attorneys, ESOP consultants, etc. If the CPA does not involve other experts, it may behoove the business owner to request it.

If, based upon this initial exploration process, the business owner decides to investigate whether an ESOP would best accomplish his planning goals, he should hire an ESOP consultant to prepare an ESOP Feasibility Analysis. A Feasibility Analysis serves dual purposes:

- It will provide the business owner and other key decision makers all of the information they need to make an informed decision whether to implement an ESOP, and
- It will serve as a road map to help guide the parties through the ESOP implementation process.

Assuming that the decision makers like what they see in the Feasibility Study, I recommend that they allow us to arrange discussions with a valuation consultant and with potential bank lenders. While our Feasibility Study contains predictive data on these two subjects, I believe it is critical to get definitive commitments on valuation and financing prior to incurring or committing to any other ESOP implementation expenses.

Please note that neither the company nor its owner(s) should engage the valuation consultant. As noted at several points earlier in this book, the law requires that the valuation consultant be independent. This is best achieved by having the ESOP trustee hire a valuation consultant who has no prior relationship with the company or its owner(s).

Once the company has decided that an ESOP is the appropriate ownership succession planning strategy and the company has a valuation and financing structure it is comfortable with, it is time to assemble the ESOP team. The team typically will consist of:

- The company's owner(s) and successor management team;
- The company's attorney and CPA;
- The ESOP consultant;
- The ESOP attorney;
- The bank that will finance the purchase;
- The ESOP trustee, and
- The owner(s)' financial advisor.

The attorneys and ESOP consultant will be involved in the preparation of the following documents:

- The ESOP Plan, Trust and Summary Plan Description;
- The stock sales agreement;
- The Inside Loan agreements and related documents;
- Opinions of Counsel;
- Post-sales employment agreements, and
- An Equity-Based Incentive Plan for the Company's successor management team.

The attorneys also will be responsible for reviewing and negotiating the bank loan agreements.

The ESOP consultant will be responsible for coordinating a Plan Administration firm that will administer the ESOP and 401k. Most companies that adopt an ESOP already have a 401k plan and it is important that the two plans be operated by a single plan administrator. The consultant also will be responsible for creating an Employee Communication program designed to help the employees understand what the ESOP is, how it will operate and how it will benefit them.

The time and cost involved in implementing an ESOP are dependent upon several factors. If the ESOP will be unleveraged, the entire plan could be structured and implemented within 30-45 days and could cost as little as $25,000. If the ESOP will be leveraged using Seller Notes only (no bank debt) the plan could be structured and implemented within 60-120 days and cost as little as $50,000. If the ESOP will be leveraged using bank debt and Seller Notes (the most common structure) the plan could be implemented within 90-180 days and cost $100,000+. Please note that these estimates are all-inclusive and consider legal, valuation and trustee fees.

I am frequently asked how the cost of implementing an ESOP compares to the cost of other succession planning options. In my experience an ESOP is less expensive than a sale to Outsiders or Insiders.

Sales to Outsiders generally involve investment bankers or business brokers who typically charge a fee that is a percentage of the sales price. If you are selling your company for $10 million, you may pay an investment banker $400,000 (4%) and pay attorney, accounting and other fees of $50,000-$100,000. A $10 million ESOP transaction may have total fees of $200,000. This is less than half the cost of selling to an Outsider.

The professional fees involved in selling to Insiders may be very low; perhaps as little as $25,000. However, as detailed in Chapter 2, there are very significant tax costs involved in selling to Insiders. Generally, a sale to Insiders will have a tax cost of at least 50%. Therefore, on a $10 million sale to Insiders the tax cost will be $5 million, approximately 25 times the total cost involved in implementing an ESOP.

GLOSSARY

Accumulated earnings

Profits generated by a company that are not distributed to the company's owners but are either reinvested in the company or kept as a reserve. The IRS monitors the accumulation of earnings in a corporation to make sure that the accumulated earnings are reasonable both in terms of the amount and purposes for which they are being accumulated. A legitimate reason to accumulate earnings would be to cover a repurchase liability obligation; an unacceptable reason a company might limit its dividend payout would be to reduce the amount of income stockholders' must declare.

Adequate consideration

This is the fair market value of a share of a privately held company. Since the company is not publicly traded, its value can't be determined by reference to a stock quote. Thus, the trustee or fiduciary of the ESOP will hire an independent appraiser to determine what a share is worth.

Advance rates

A lender may offer an advance (loan) against assets, setting a certain percentage for the advance depending on what the asset is; e.g., receivables, tangible assets, etc. For example, a lender may have an advance rate of 85% against accounts receivable.

Air-ball loan

A loan made that exceeds the amount of collateral put up. It is usually paid off within two years. For example, if a company needs a $10 million loan but only has collateral with an advance rate of $8 million, the air-ball would be $2 million.

Allocation

The process of dividing or apportioning stock among ESOP participants' accounts. Typically, allocations are made on a salary ratio basis. For example, if a participant's pay equals 1 percent of the pay of all eligible plan participants' pay, that participant would receive 1 percent of the shares allocated that year.

Amortization

The periodic repayment of a loan typically in equal installments which include interest and principal.

Annual addition

In a defined contribution plan, this is the total amount of employer contributions, forfeitures and employee contributions allocated to a participant's account. There are limits to the amount that can be allocated; however, these do change for reasons such as cost of living increases. ESOP dividends or distributions paid to participants are not considered additions.

Appreciation

An increase in value of an asset such as a stock, bond, commodity or real estate.

Balloon payment

Some loans are written with a balloon payment, meaning that the initial payments are kept lower by adding a substantially higher payment required at the end of the loan period.

Basis

The value of an asset used for computing gain or loss when the asset is sold. Tax basis generally equals the asset's purchase price less accumulated depreciation.

Beneficial owner

When an ESOP holds employer securities in the ESOP trust, the trustee holds the title and is the legal owner; however, the participants are the beneficial owners, meaning they participate in the benefits of ownership even though the title is in another name.

Book value

An asset's net value shown on the company's balance sheet. Book value is calculated by deducting accumulated depreciation from the purchase price of the asset.

Buy-sell agreement

A legally binding agreement between owners to buy or sell ownership interests in a company – in a corporation, its stock.

C Corporation

This is a corporation in which both the corporation and the shareholders pay tax on income: the corporation pays tax on income and the shareholders pay tax on the dividends. Under certain guidelines, an ESOP offers tax-deductible dividends to the company, whereas all other dividends in C corporations are nondeductible.

Capital expenditure

Investment made to purchase new capital assets or to improve existing ones. Often referred to as "CAPEX."

Capital gains tax

Tax payable on profit made from the sale of a capital asset. Often, profits on capital assets held for 12 months or longer are taxed at a lower rate.

Capitalization factor *(see capitalization rate)*

This is a multiple used to convert income into value.

Capitalization rate

The discount (or interest) rate used to determine the present value of anticipated future cash receipts.

Carry forward

A tax benefit that results from offsetting one period's loss versus another period's gain. The carry forward refers to a loss being carried over to another year rather than being taken in the current year.

Carryback

For federal income tax purposes, the portion of a net operating loss deductible from net income of the prior three years. This amount is absorbed and the remainder carried forward to offset future years' net income.

Cash flow

The difference between cash available at the beginning of a period (opening balance) and the amount at the end of the period (closing balance).

Charitable remainder trust (CRT)

An arrangement through which a donor receives income for a period (either a specified number of years or for life) from an asset donated to a charity. Upon the termination of the trust (at the end of the specified period or upon the donor's death), the charity has all rights to the donated asset.

Cliff vesting

A provision of a retirement plan that specifies that employer contributions to participants' accounts become the property of the participants all at once rather than gradually. A retirement plan can have either a graduated vesting schedule under which participants become vested in their accounts incrementally over a 6-year period or a cliff vesting schedule under which there is no vesting during years 1-3, and participants become 100% vested on the first day of the fourth year.

Closely held company

This is a private company whose shares are owned by individuals or small groups and is not subject to the regulations that govern publicly owned companies.

Collateral

Assets, either tangible or intangible, pledged as security for loan.

Common law employees

A person who provides services for a company, typically on a full-time basis, but is not an owner of the company or an independent contractor. Common law employees that satisfy a retirement plan's eligibility requirements, become participants in the plan.

Common stock

Represents equity ownership in a corporation, providing voting rights and entitling the holder to dividends and/or capital appreciation. In the event of a liquidation of the corporation, common stockholders are paid any value that remains after the company's debt holders and preferred shareholders have been paid.

Compensation

Salary, wages, bonuses, overtime pay or commissions paid to employees by the employer.

Compound interest

Interest computed on the principal to which interest earned to-date has been added, resulting in the investment growing exponentially as opposed to linearly as in the case of simple interest.

Contribution limits

Limits on the amount either an employee or employer may contribute to a retirement plan. These limits are contained in Section 415 of the Internal Revenue Code and, therefore, are also referred to as the "415 limits."

Control

The ability to direct how a company is managed. The term often refers to an individual or group holding "controlling interest," meaning they have greater power than other owners to make decisions.

Controlled group

Corporations grouped together for tax purposes. The groups may be through such relationships as parent-subsidiary organizations or a brother-sister controlled group. The Controlled Group rules require closely related companies to be treated as a single employer for retirement plan purposes. This means that employees of all the related companies must be considered when applying the IRS coverage and discrimination tests.

Corporate governance

This system organizes the responsibilities, privileges and authority of a company's shareholders, board of directors and management. In a traditional system, the shareholders elect the directors of the company and vote on high level corporate matters such as acquisitions, mergers, and so on. The board of directors hires management and holds them accountable for the company's health and success. Management runs the company's day-to-day operations.

Corporate Owned Life Insurance (COLI)

Corporations sometimes purchase life insurance on "key persons" who are integral to the success of the corporation. The corporation is the beneficiary of these policies. This action is to guard against the cost of losing key executives to unexpected death and having to invest sizable sums to fund corporate obligations or to recruit and train qualified replacements.

Corporate stock

An ownership share of a corporation. There are different classes and categories of stock: common, preferred or classified, and they may be issued, unissued or issued and subsequently repurchased.

Corporation

A business legally organized under state and federal law as a separate entity having its own rights, responsibilities, liability and tax requirements.

Covenant

An agreement between a buyer and a seller that each will behave within certain guidelines and standards. Such an agreement may relate to providing financial information, conducting business, maintaining current practices and so on.

Coverage ratio

It is the amount of a liability compared with the company's ability to pay. For example, if a company has a $10 million loan (its liability) and has annual cash flow (EBITDA) of $3.5 million, its coverage ratio would be 2.81 to 1. The lower the ratio, the better.

Covered payroll

Total compensation of all the participants covered under a retirement plan.

Cumulative dividend

A dividend that accumulates if not paid in the period when due and must be paid in full before other dividends are paid on the Company's common stock.

Debt capacity

Assessment of the amount of debt a company can repay in a timely manner without jeopardizing its financial viability.

Debt service

Payment of principal and interest on a loan on a regular schedule.

Deemed-owned shares

When testing for the ESOP anti-abuse rules (409(p) testing), the following are considered owned or deemed owned shares: shares allocated to the individual's ESOP account, unallocated shares that will be allocated to the individual as the ESOP loan is paid off, and the individual's share of synthetic equity, including stock options and warrants, phantom stock, stock appreciation rights and other forms of deferred compensation.

Default

Failure to live up to a legal obligation, such as failure to pay financial debts. In the case of ESOP, the plan's failure to service its ESOP loan(s).

Deferred compensation

Remuneration that is paid out in an accounting period later than the accounting period in which the remuneration was awarded. In a "deferred compensation plan," payment of a portion of the salary or bonus earned by an employee in a current period may be postponed until the employee's retirement. If properly structured, taxation of the amount deferred will be postponed until it is paid.

Defined benefit pension plan

A type of qualified retirement plan in which an employer promises a specific monthly benefit to employees upon retirement. The benefit amount is predetermined using a formula based upon the employer's earnings history, tenure of service and age. The employer bears the investment risk.

Defined contribution plan

A type of qualified retirement plan in which the amount of the employer's annual contribution is specified. Individual accounts are established for plan participants and retirement benefits are based on the amounts contributed to the accounts plus any investment earnings. The employees bear the investment risk.

Depreciation

Generally speaking, a company's fixed assets (such as equipment or a facility) decrease in value over time as a result of normal wear and tear. According to GAAP (General Accepted Accounting Principles), the company does not deduct the asset's total cost at the time of purchase, but, rather, spreads the cost out over its useful lifetime. The company's income statement reports the amount of reduction each year until it is completely written off.

Determination letter

A company may file an application with the IRS requesting acknowledgement that a pension, profit-sharing or ESOP meets the requirements of the Internal Revenue Code. When the IRS is satisfied that the plan meets those requirements, it will issue a determination letter.

Discount factor

The interest rate that translates expected benefits or costs in any given future year into present value terms.

Discount rate
The interest rate charged by the Federal Revenue Bank (the "Fed") on cash loans to member banks.

Discounted cash flow
A company's anticipated future cash flows expressed back to today's dollars using a discount factor.

Disqualified persons
A term used in conjunction with S-corporation ESOP Anti-Abuse testing (Section 409(p)). The term refers to a person who owns 10% or more of an S-corporation's "deemed – owned shares" (20% or more considering the family attribution rules). See Chapter 13, Q&As 27-43.

Distributions
The disbursement of a participant's vested ESOP account following a distributable event including death, retirement, disability or termination of employment.

Diversification
ESOPs must provide certain participants the opportunity to convert the employer stock in their ESOP account into other investments. See Chapter 11, Q&As 13-21.

Dividend deduction
Under Section 404(k) of the Internal Revenue Code, C-corporations can get a tax deduction for dividends paid on ESOP owned shares if: they are used to repay an ESOP loan, are passed through to participants or are reinvested by participants in ESOP shares. The amount that is deductible is limited to the amount of a "reasonable" dividend.

Earnings before Interest, Taxes, Depreciation and Amortization (EBITDA)
An approximate measure of a company's operating cash flow.

Eligible payroll

Generally means total compensation paid to those employees who satisfy a retirement plan's eligibility requirement. An employer may contribute to its ESOP or other qualified retirement plan a certain percentage of eligible payroll.

Employee Retirement Income Security Act of 1974, as amended (ERISA)

This is the law that governs how retirement plans work. Enacted in 1974, it defines the rules employers must comply with in order to reap the tax benefits of offering a "qualified retirement plan." See Chapter 8.

Employee Stock Ownership Plan (ESOP)

A defined contribution retirement plan that gives employees a financial interest in the company by virtue of their ownership of stock contributed by the employer. An ESOP is required to invest primarily in the stock of the company that sponsors the plan.

Employee Stock Ownership Trust (ESOT)

The legal entity that owns the assets of an Employee Stock Ownership Plan (ESOP). ESOTs are tax-exempt trusts.

Equity

Ownership interest in a corporation in the form of common or preferred stock.

ESOP rollover

Under IRC Section 1042, a shareholder defers the tax liability from any gain received from the sale of qualifying employer securities to an ESOP. The ESOP must own at least 30% of the value of the company's stock immediately after the sale, and the proceeds of the sale must be reinvested in qualified replacement property within a 15-month period beginning three months prior to the sale. See Chapter 10.

ESOT

See Employee Stock Ownership Trust.

Estate equalization

Strategies by which parents can equalize the value of the inheritance left to children regardless of whether the children are active in the family business.

Exempt loan

Unlike other types of qualified retirement plans that are barred from borrowing money, ESOPs are allowed to borrow money to purchase qualifying employer securities. There are certain conditions that must be met. See Chapter 9.

Fair market value

This is the value of a property as defined by what an informed buyer (given reasonable facts) would pay and an informed seller (also with reasonable facts) would accept, under the condition that neither is compelled by circumstances to buy or sell.

Fairness opinion

An opinion of the fairness of the terms of a proposed transaction written by an independent party, such as an investment banking or valuation firm.

Feasibility study

When an ESOP is being considered, a full feasibility study is conducted to see if it is likely to succeed. It would include comprehensive financial analysis covering valuation, stockholders' equity analysis, design study and liquidity report. See online appendix (www.esopcoach.com) for sample ESOP Feasibility Study.

Fiduciary

A person or group – such as trustees, plan administrators or corporate directors – authorized to exercise discretionary control over ESOP plan administration, investments, management or plan assets.

Fiduciary liability

Like the fiduciaries of any employee benefit plan, ESOP fiduciaries are responsible for losses resulting from their failure to carry out their duties. In an ESOP, however, fiduciaries enjoy certain exemptions that allow them to invest primarily in employer securities and to enter into exempt loans.

Flow through

In a flow-through entity the company's income passes straight through to the owners who pay the tax on the income. This eliminates the entity from paying taxes. An S corporation is an example of a flow-through entity. See Chapter 11.

Forfeiture

A forfeiture generally means giving up certain privileges or assets if you fail to meet contractual obligations. As it relates to an ESOP, it means the non-vested amount of an employee's account that the employee does not receive when his employment terminates. The "forfeited" amount is reallocated among remaining participants.

401k plan

A qualified retirement plan which permits pre-tax contributions from employees and percentage matches by employers (such as dollar-for-dollar). Employees are not taxed on contributions until the time of distribution.

Free cash flow

Money available for the company after all obligations have been satisfied.

Golden handcuffs

Incentives such as stock options with long vesting periods designed to retain key management by making it financially disadvantageous for them to leave.

Highly compensated employee

A highly compensated employee is one who is a member of the company's top-paid group; one who held a 5% ownership and received compensation in excess of a set amount during the preceding year.

Holding company

A company created to hold stock in operating subsidiaries.

Hour of service

Any hour of an employee's time for which the company pays, whether it is for regular work-week hours, overtime, paid holidays, sick leave or vacation.

Hypothecation

Pledging assets as collateral for a loan.

Independent appraiser

A qualified, experienced appraiser chosen to value shares in connection with an ESOP. This individual or group should have no ties to the company for which it is conducting the share appraisal. See Chapter 12.

Independent professional valuation

In the course of creating an ESOP, there must be a determination of the worth of the company. This is done by an independent, unbiased, professional valuation firm.

Insiders

When an owner wants to sell a business, he may choose to sell to insiders, meaning key employees or family members.

Internal Revenue Code (IRC)

Federal statutes that govern the taxation of individuals, corporations and other entities.

Investment bank

Financial institution with special expertise in financing sources and structures which performs preparatory and implementation services for clients seeking assistance with mergers and acquisitions or transaction financing.

IRC

See Internal Revenue Code.

Key employee

An individual whose knowledge, reputation and/or skills are critical to the continuing success of a company and whose loss may damage the company. Key employees often are offered special financial incentives (often referred to as SARs or MSOPs) to remain with the company.

KSOP

A combination 401k plan and ESOP. This is a plan in which employer matching contributions and employee contributions may be used to acquire stock or repay ESOP indebtedness.

Lending memorandum

A document used to request proposals from lenders to finance a specific transaction such as an ESOP's acquisition of employer securities. Typically prepared by an investment banker or ESOP consultant, it contains detailed financial information about the company and specifies the loan terms the borrower would like.

Leverage ratio

Measure of a company's leverage and its capacity for debt repayment. It is calculated by dividing total debt by owner's equity.

Leveraged buyout (LBO)

A purchaser borrows money to purchase a company, using the company's assets as security for the loan. After the purchase, the loan is paid from the purchased company's cash flow.

Leveraged ESOP

An ESOP that acquires qualifying employer securities using borrowed funds.

LIBOR

London InterBank Offered Rate of interest. The interest rate that banks charge on loans to one another.

Limitation year

The 12-month period defined in a retirement plan for testing its compliance with IRS requirements. It is the plan year unless the employer elects to use any other consecutive 12-month period.

Line of credit

A fixed amount of credit available to a company for a certain period of time. A lending institution and customer agree to terms and conditions in advance.

Loan agreement

A legal document that evidences a loan. It covers the amount of the loan, the interest rate, repayment terms, covenants and the borrower's representations of the business.

Loan commitment

A document transmitted to a borrower from a lender in which the lender agrees to loan money to the borrower under certain terms specified in the document, often referred to as a "commitment letter."

Loan facility

A loan or collection of loans taken by a corporation. These loans may include letters of credit and term loans.

Long-term debt

Liabilities that extend beyond one year.

Lump-sum distribution

A one-time payment of the entire retirement plan (ESOP) account balance. Under certain conditions lump-sum distributions may be receive special tax treatment. See Chapter 14, Q&As, 17-26.

Majority stockholder

An individual or entity that owns more than 50% of a corporation's voting stock.

Management buyout (MBO)

The purchase of a company or one of its divisions by the existing management, usually with outside financing.

Marketability discount

A percentage deducted from the value of closely held company stock because closely held stock cannot be sold as easily as the stock of a publicly traded company.

Mezzanine financing

Non-conventional funding that shares characteristics of both debt and equity. It may include mezzanine debt which is subordinated to senior debt and carries a significantly higher rate of interest than senior debt. It may also include equity-based options such as warrants.

Minority interest discount

A percentage deducted from the value of a block of shares of a closely held company because they represent 50% or less of the voting power and, therefore, cannot control the company.

Minority interest

An individual or entity that owns less than 50% of the voting interest in a company.

Net operating loss (NOL)

The amount by which net operating expenses exceed operating revenue in an accounting period.

Net present value (NPV)

A formula that allows analysts to anticipate a potential desired rate of return by looking at the current value of cash inflow minus outflow, taking into account a current discount rate.

Net worth

On a company's balance sheet, the remainder of assets minus liabilities.

Noncallable convertible preferred stock

A preferred stock which can be converted into common stock at the option of the shareholder (convertible) and which can only be redeemed by payment to the shareholder of a penalty such as it being converted to common stock when called (non-callable). An ESOP can purchase this type of employer security.

Non-leveraged ESOP

An ESOP that does not use loans to acquire employer stock. Typically, the company contributes cash to the ESOP which it uses to purchase stock from existing shareholders.

Note

A legal document in which the "maker" (the borrower) promises to pay a specified amount to the "payee" (the lender) on demand or on a stated date(s). Also referred to as a "promissory note."

Open book management

The practice of sharing relevant financial information about the company with employees so that they can understand the importance of their actions on the performance of the company and can make better decisions as workers.

Operating corporation

For purposes of Section 1042 "qualified replacement property," a corporation with no more than 25% passive income and that uses at least 50% of its income to operate a trade or business. See Chapter 10, Q&A 10.

Outsiders

In the context of "selling to outsiders," "outsiders" refers to people who are not family members of the seller and who do not work for the company ("insiders"). Outsiders include strategic and financial buyers, among others.

Ownership culture

The decision by management to promote distribution of equity to employees, creating a mindset of ownership and ultimately leading to greater employee dedication and performance for the good of the company.

Participant

An employee who meets ERISA requirements for participation in an ESOP and the plan specifications, usually meaning a certain length of employment and a certain number of hours within a given period.

Party in interest

An individual specified by ERISA who is prohibited from making certain transactions involving a retirement plan. Parties in interest may include: the employer and its owners, and officers, trustees, among others.

Pass-through of voting rights

In closely held companies the ESOP trustee must follow participant directions when voting allocated shares on several major corporate issues including: liquidation, sale of all or substantially all of the company's assets, recapitalization, merger and related issues. This is referred to as the pass-through of voting rights. See Chapter 13, Q&As 13-17.

Pension Protection Act (PPA)

Signed into law in 2006, it is the most comprehensive pension reform legislation since ERISA was enacted in 1974. The Act, which comprises approximately 400 pages, will lead to many changes in the way companies operate their retirement plans. However, the Act did not make major changes to the rules governing ESOPs.

Plan document

The document that defines all the rules and procedures of the ESOP. It may be filed with the IRS with a request for a determination letter.

Preferred stock

A class of stock that pays fixed and regular dividends (such as 6% of the amount paid for each share). The dividend typically is cumulative (see "cumulative dividends"). Holders of preferred stock have claim over the company's earnings (and assets in case of liquidation) ahead of the claim of holders of common stock but behind the claims of bond holders and other creditors. Preferred shares generally cost more (have greater value) than common stock.

Prefunding

In anticipation of an ESOP's repurchase obligation, the company may make additional cash contributions to the ESOP or accumulate money within the company.

Prepayment penalty

A charge assessed for paying off a loan in advance of its due date.

Present value

An amount that must be invested to create either an ongoing income or a lump sum at a future date. The amount is determined using the company's cost of capital, typically, the rate at which it borrows money.

Pre-tax dollars

Prior to calculating income and taxes, certain income may be deducted, thus creating the advantage of a lower amount of taxable income. In an ESOP, dollars that are contributed by the company are deducted from the company's taxable income; i.e., pre-tax dollars.

Prime rate

The rate a lender charges its preferred corporate customers.

Private equity group (PEG)

Private equity is an asset class consisting of securities in operating companies that are not publically traded. Types of private equity include leveraged buyout, venture capital, growth capital, distressed and special situations, mezzanine capital, etc. Private equity groups

(PEGs) raise, invest and distribute their private equity funds.

Professional Employer Organization (PEO)

Provides outsourcing of payroll, workers' compensation, human resource and employee benefits by hiring a client company's employees, thus becoming their employer of record.

Profit

Proceeds amounting to the difference between total sales and the cost of making the sales and operating the business.

Profit-sharing plan

An individual account, qualified defined contribution retirement plan. The company can make contributions (at its discretion) to employee accounts where the contributions are invested, typically based upon the employee's direction. If the profit sharing plan includes 401k provisions, the employees can make pre-tax contributions to the plan which the employer may match.

Prohibited transaction

A transaction between a plan and a disqualified person that is prohibited by law. Prohibited transactions generally include the following transactions:

- A transfer of plan income or assets to, or use of them by, or for the benefit of a disqualified person;
- Any act of a fiduciary by which plan income or assets are used for his or her own interest;
- The receipt of consideration by a fiduciary for his or her own account from any party dealing with the plan in a transaction that involves plan income or assets;
- The sale, exchange or lease of property between a plan and a disqualified person;

- Lending money or extending credit between a plan and a disqualified person;
- Furnishing goods, services or facilities between a plan and a disqualified person.

The Department of Labor has granted "class exemptions" for certain types of investments under conditions that protect the safety and security of plan assets. In addition, plan sponsors may apply to the Department of Labor for a prohibited transaction exemption.

ESOPs are exempt from a number of ERISA's prohibited transaction rules. For example, in an ESOP transaction a "disqualified person" (a shareholder) can sell company stock to the ESOT and the ESOT can borrow money and issue promissory notes to selling shareholders in exchange for their stock.

Promissory note

An agreement to pay an amount on demand or by a specific date.

Prudence rule

It originates from the 1830 ruling of Judge Samuel Putnam that: "Those with responsibility to invest money for others should act with prudence, discretion, intelligence and regard for the safety of capital as well as income."

Put

The right but not the obligation for the holder of an asset to sell it in the future for a set price.

Qualified domestic relation order (QDRO)

A court order that creates or recognizes the existence of an alternate payee's (a divorced spouse's) right to receive all or a portion of the benefits payable with respect to a participant under a retirement plan.

Qualified plan

A plan that meets the requirements of Internal Revenue Code Section 401(a) and is thus eligible for favorable tax treatment. See Chapter 8 for detail regarding "requirements."

Qualified Replacement Property (QRP)

Stocks, bonds, debentures, warrants or other debt or equity instruments issued by U.S. corporations that receive not more than 25% of their income from passive investments. U.S. companies are companies controlled by U.S. firms, not simply companies with operating units in the U.S. and listed on U.S. stock exchanges (Schlumberger or Food Lion, for instance, would be foreign firms). Mutual funds, U.S. government and municipal bonds, for instance, do not qualify, but banks and insurance companies do. The company can be public or private and can be owned by the seller to the ESOP. It cannot be owned by the company sponsoring the ESOP. See Chapter 10, Q&As 10-19.

Qualifying employer securities

Only certain types of securities are allowed to be purchased by an ESOP and receive favorable tax treatment. These include readily tradable common stock, certain types of convertible preferred stock and stock that has a combination of voting and dividend rights at least equal to the most favorable voting rights.

Reallocate

Redistribute non-vested forfeited shares in an ESOP.

Recapitalization

A change in a company's capital structure, such as an exchange of stocks for bonds or the creation of additional shares.

Recourse

A recourse loan is one for which the borrower has personal liability. The lender's recourse in the event of default stretches beyond the collateral pledged by the borrower and includes his personal assets.

Recycle or recycling

When participants receive the benefit of the ESOP shares but the stock either remains in the trust or is distributed to the participant and then repurchased by the trust. There are three ways a recycle may take place. First, the participant receives cash and the stock never leaves the trust. Shares are reallocated to remaining participants' accounts. Second, the stock is distributed, the company buys it and re-contributes it to the ESOP. Third, the ESOP distributes the shares and then repurchases them.

Redemption

The reacquisition of a security by the company that issued the security. For example, when a participant has a distributable event, the company sponsoring the ESOP may redeem shares and retire them as treasury stock.

Refinancing

Retiring debt by issuing new debt or equity securities, usually with the purpose of reducing interest costs.

Replacement period

In the context of a Section 1042 exchange, the 15-month period that begins three months prior to the sale to the ESOP and that ends 12 months following the sale.

Representations and warranties

In stock purchase agreements (and other transaction documents), buyers and sellers make specific representations and warranties to each other. These are statements by which one party gives assurances to the other regarding certain facts that are essential to the transaction. Often there are specific remedies if the representations and warranties are not accurate or are not fulfilled. Because of the consequences of making representations and warranties, parties typically try to limit the number and scope of the ones they make.

Repurchase obligation

One of the main purposes of an ESOP is to provide benefits to the participants. Because of this, companies must provide a mechanism for participants to realize the value of the stock held in their account. Section 409(h) of the Internal Revenue Code requires that a closely held company sponsoring an ESOP buy the stock back from participants who receive distributions from the plan. This legal requirement is known as the "repurchase obligation."

Rescue ESOP

An ESOP established by a company that is in desperate financial condition. They often involve wage and benefit concessions by employees and very aggressive/risky financing structures. Examples include United Airlines, Weirton Steel and The Tribune Company.

Right of first refusal

When ESOP securities have been distributed to participants or beneficiaries and they propose to transfer the securities to a third party, the ESOP or employer has the first option to purchase them.

Rollover

A tax-deferred transfer of cash or securities from one qualified plan or individual retirement account to another qualified plan or individual retirement account.

S Corporation

A "flow-through" entity, meaning that the company does not pay income tax. Rather, its earnings flow through to its shareholders who pay tax on the company's earnings.

Securities

Items related to ownership of an entity including stocks, bonds, debentures, etc.

Securities acquisition loan

A loan used to acquire qualifying employer securities for an ESOP.

Security

In the context of investments, a security signifies evidence of debt or equity of a company. Examples include stocks, bonds, options and futures. In the context of lending, the pledging of assets to guaranty the repayment of a loan.

Security interest

A creditor's claim against a debtor's assets; the assets may be sold to satisfy the debtor's obligation.

Seller note or seller paper

A note payable to the seller as part of the purchase price, and typically subordinated to the debt of senior lenders.

Senior debt

This is debt that will be paid back first from proceeds of a liquidation in the event of a loan default. Debt that is paid before subordinated debt.

Shareholders/stockholders

Individuals, groups, institutions, trusts or others who own shares of stock representing ownership of a company.

Sinking fund

A cash fund set aside to pay a liability that comes due at a later date. For example, a company might create a sinking fund to pay for an ESOP's repurchase obligation.

SPD

See Summary Plan Description.

Sponsor

As it relates to an ESOP, the sponsor is the company that adopts the ESOP plan. In another sense, it is a party interested in supporting or financing a project.

Stepped-up basis

Under the estate tax law, a provision that allows the tax basis of an asset to be determined by the asset's market value at the time of the owner's death.

Stock

A share of ownership in a corporation.

Stock appreciation rights (SAR)

Stock appreciation rights refer to an executive's ability to receive cash or stock equal to the amount by which the firm's stock price exceeds a specified base price.

Stock bonus plan

A qualified profit sharing retirement plan in which a company contributes stock to participants' accounts rather than cash.

Stock option

A right granted for a certain number of years to purchase stock at a set price.

Stock redemption

Repurchase of shares by the issuing corporation.

Subordinated debt

Debt that, in the case of liquidation, is repaid secondarily to that of senior debt.

Subordination agreement

A document that specifies which debt will be paid off first, that is, which lender's claim takes precedence over another's.

Summary plan description (SPD)

A description of the retirement plan's provisions that legally must be distributed to all plan participants.

Suspense account

In a leveraged ESOP, all shares acquired with loan proceeds are initially held in the ESOP's suspense account. Shares are transferred from the suspense account as the loan is repaid and are allocated to individual participant's accounts.

Synthetic equity

In the context of the S Corporation ESOP Anti-Abuse rules (Section 409(p)), includes stock options, stock appreciation rights and other equity equivalents broadly defined to include, for example, deferred compensation and split dollar plans.

Tag-along right

A right that protects minority shareholders by giving them assurance that if the majority shareholder sells his stake, minority shareholders have the right to sell on the same terms and conditions as would apply to the majority shareholder.

Tax deduction

Costs associated with doing business are deducted from a company's taxable income, resulting in tax savings.

Tax deferral

Paying taxes in the future on income earned in the current year. In a 401k plan or ESOP, participants do not pay tax on the earnings of their accounts until their accounts are distributed to them.

Tax-deferred rollover

In the context of a distribution from a qualified retirement plan, refers to a tax-free reinvestment of the distribution into an IRA or other qualified plan, usually within 60 days.

In the context of a sale of C-corporation stock to an ESOP, tax-deferred rollover refers to the ability of the seller to defer taxation of his sales proceeds if he reinvests them in accordance with Section 1042 of the Internal Revenue Code. See Chapter 10.

Tender offer

A formal, time-specified offer to shareholders to acquire the outstanding shares of a corporation for cash or securities.

Term loan

A loan with a maturity longer than one-year.

Trustee

The person or institution that holds an ESOP's assets and acts as a plan fiduciary.

Uniformed Services Employment and Reemployment Rights Act (USERRA)

This act governs employer obligations to employees on military leave.

Unrelated Business Income Tax (UBIT)

Income earned by a tax-exempt entity that does not result from its tax-exempt activities is subject to this tax.

Unsecured loan

A loan granted solely on the general credit of the borrower as evidenced by the balance sheet and management's proven ability.

Valuation

In the context of an ESOP, the process for determining the price the ESOP will pay for the selling shareholder(s)' stock and the price of the stock each year to be used in calculating the value of a participant's ESOP account.

Valuation discounts

When assessing the value of a company, certain discounts are applied for issues such as lack of control or lack of marketability.

Vesting

The process during which participants gain full ownership (non-forfeitable interest) of their ESOP account balances. Vesting may occur in percentages after certain periods of service or it may occur at a specified time, such as retirement.

Warrant

A security, usually with a limited life, that authorizes the holder to purchase shares of common stock at a specified price. A warrant's life is usually longer than the life of an option. Warrants are sometimes offered to investors for their financial risk.

AFTERWORD

Baby Boomer Business Owners, I challenge you to take charge of your Ownership Succession Planning. Don't wait until there is a crisis and your planning options are limited.

Your company will be a critical component of your personal legacy. Don't leave it to chance.

You will need help with this planning process. Turn to the advisors you know and trust to begin the process.

Call or email if I can be your ESOP Coach.

Kelly O. Finnell, J.D., CLU, AIF®
Executive Financial Services, Inc.
7660 Poplar Pike, 2nd Floor
Germantown, TN 38138
Phone 901-259-7979
Fax 901-682-8653
kfin@execfin.com

AUTHOR BIO

Kelly Finnell is one of the nation's premier ESOP and Ownership Succession Planning consultants and one of the most sought-after speakers on this subject. He has spoken at more than 200 conferences and meetings throughout the U.S. and in London, England, and Sydney, Australia, and has published numerous articles on the use of ESOPs in Ownership Succession Planning. Kelly has spent his entire professional career (more than 25 years) helping small to midsize business owners design and execute succession strategies and ESOPs.

Kelly is a member of the Business Enterprise Institute (BEI), the nation's leading organization of Exit Planning professionals; M Financial Group, one of the nation's leading independent financial services companies, the National Center for Employee Ownership (NCEO) and The ESOP Association.

Kelly graduated from the University of Memphis (magna cum laude) and from its Law School, where he was published in the Law Review, served as Chief Justice of the Moot Court Board, received the American Jurisprudence Award for Equitable Remedies, was the recipient of the Judge John D. Martin Scholarship and was named to Who's Who in American Colleges and Universities. Kelly has earned the Accredited Investment Fiduciary™ professional designation, awarded by the Center for Fiduciary Studies, which is associated with the University of Pittsburgh.

Kelly has served in leadership roles in numerous professional and community activities, including: President of the Memphis Chapter of the Society of Financial Services Professionals, Vestry Member and Treasurer of his church, President of Family Services of Memphis, as a member of the Board of Directors of Renasant Bank and of the Economic Club of Memphis and on the Dean's Advisory Council at the Christian Brothers University School of Business.

APPENDIX A

Ownership Succession Planning Matrix

	Sell to Outsiders	Sell to Insiders	Till Death Do Us Part	ESOP Innovation
Taxation	15% - 40%	50%	40%-50%	0%-15%
Control	None	Some	Max	Substantial
Perqs	Limited	Substantial	Max	Substantial
Upfront Cash	Max	Limited	None	Substantial
Income	Minimal	Substantial	Max	Substantial
Involvement	Minimal	Substantial	Max	You Decide!
Kids/Keys	None	Max	Delayed	Substantial
Employee Incentive	Minimal	Substantial	Minimal	Max
Corp. Taxation	Traditional	Traditional	Traditional	Tax-Free!

ESOP COACH

INDEX